SUCCEED IN REAL ESTATE WITHOUT COLD CALLING

Learn How to Earn
$100,000 Your First Year
Selling Real Estate!

SUCCEED IN REAL ESTATE WITHOUT COLD CALLING

If You Hate to Cold Call and You're
Not a Super Salesperson, This Book
Is Destined to Be Your Bible!

Phil Gerisilo, Realtor®
Rob Lebow

SelectBooks, Inc.

Succeed in Real Estate Without Cold Calling
© 2005 by Phil Gerisilo, Realtor® and Rob Lebow

This edition published by SelectBooks, Inc., New York, New York.

First Edition

ISBN 1-59079-070-7

Library of Congress Cataloging-in-Publication Data

Gerisilo, Phil, 1952–

Succeed in real estate without cold calling : learn how to make $100,000 your first year selling real estate / Phil Gerisilo, Rob Lebow -- 1st ed.

p. cm.

"If you hate to cold call and you're not a super salesperson, this book is destined to be your bible!"

ISBN 1-59079-070-7 (hardcover : alk. paper)

1. Real estate business. 2. Real estate agents. I. Lebow, Rob. II. Title.

HD1375.G43 2005

333.33'023'73--dc22

2005014024

Printed in the United States of America

10 9 8 7 6 5 4 3 2 1   •

Greek Gods characters by David Palukaitis

WHAT THEY SAY ABOUT PHIL & ROB'S BOOK!

Phil and Rob focus on service and integrity. There is a lack of integrity in training today. I always support those who understand the meaning of that concept. Excellent insights for agents who need to learn how to work smarter and enjoy the business. I like their approach—not a phony quick fix!

Danielle Kennedy
Leading Real Estate Trainer and Author

Quality service and valued relationships are all that count in the real estate business. Succeed in Real Estate Without Cold Calling *gives you everything you need to know to develop these and other critical skills for achieving a successful real estate career.*

J. Lennox Scott
Chairman and CEO, John L. Scott Real Estate

Succeed in Real Estate Without Cold Calling *is a commonsense, consumer-focused approach to selling residential Real Estate the right way! I wish I had read this book when I started. The book does a wonderful job of sharing information and giving agents the right mindset about this important subject.* Succeed in Real Estate Without Cold Calling's *message should help eradicate past manipulative sales techniques that have caused so much harm for both agents and the public. This book's message will make a difference!*

Carla Cross, CRB, MA
National Realtor Educator of the Year
Author of *Become Tomorrow's Mega-Agent Today*
and *Up and Running in 30 Days*

I think this would be an excellent book for a broker to give to their new salespeople. In this way the person could get acquainted with Phil's views to show that it is possible to be successful in their first year, while still being able to instruct them in office policies.

Yvonne Taylor
Former State Director, Yuma (AZ) Association of Realtors

Phil and Rob's book is a "must read" for all Real Estate agents, regardless of how long they've been in business. The timeless principles contained here have enabled me to successfully serve clients with joy and integrity. Thank you, Phil and Rob, for helping me launch my Real Estate career.

John Messer
Top 5% agent, the second year in the business

The book is easily read and entertaining! It was easy to identify with Mar and then to have solutions given that I could make work in the business.

Janie Stanford
Broker, Educator, Speaker

I thought Phil Gerisilo's book was enjoyable to read and easy to follow because of the conversational format. I read this book while studying for my real estate exam. I appreciate having this information before I go to work in an office where the "experienced" agents might send me in the wrong direction. Succeed in Real Estate Without Cold Calling *gives me the confidence to get started in the real estate business and know I can be successful right away!*

Dale Carlson
New Real Estate Agent

I have been encouraged by reading your book. Putting our client's needs before our own is the right formula to grow a business that is both personally and financially rewarding. Thanks for the creative way you open the minds of both new and long-time agents to creatively challenge the real estate profession.

Kent Barber
Real Estate Agent

When I met Phil for the first time I was on a motorcycle trip in Los Angeles with a large group on a benefit ride, the "Love Run." We were there a week riding up and down the coast having a great time!

A couple years had gone by since the trip when I crossed paths with Phil again. I had taken an interim job at the local Harley dealership, "Downtown Harley," as I was in the automobile business—"car sales"—for about 10 years and desperately needed a change in my life.

And what a change it was ...

Phil had asked me to consider real estate; he had also said he would bring a book in that he had written for me to read and said if I was interested he would help me. I had not considered this career, as I was leaning towards flight attendant in order to travel, until reading his book. "IT CHANGED MY LIFE!!!"

I've been an agent for over two years now and a very successful one! I am having the time of my life! This has opened up a whole new world for me. It has changed my life both financially and emotionally! I am forever indebted to Phil for this. ... He is my mentor, my role model, my lifeline! I cannot thank him enough for this opportunity. And, my daughters thank him!

When I was a child my mother always said: Things happen for a reason, they don't just happen. I think about that often. There was a reason that Phil Gerisilo walked through those doors that very day at the motorcycle dealership ... and handed me a manuscript of this book.

Marlene Bjorstad
Realtor

ACKNOWLEDGEMENTS

This book is dedicated in loving memory of my mother, Helen Gerisilo, whose life exemplified the meaning of unconditional love and the joy of serving others.

Above all, I thank God for blessing our lives so richly.

I would like to thank my good friend and co-author, Rob Lebow, for his generous contribution of time, energy, and talent to this project. Without Rob's unflagging optimism and encouragement, this book would still be just a good idea. I always look forward to spending time with Rob and the wonderful people in his office: Rob's lovely wife Sharon, and Patti and Marie. The cheerfulness, boundless energy, and eagerness to help that they offer is refreshing.

A very special thank you to our agent Bill Gladstone and to our publisher Kenzi Sugihara of Select Books for their faith in us and this book.

Thanks and love to my wife, Deborah, and our three children—Shannon, Chelsey and Nicholas—for their love and support as a family and as part of our real estate team. Without their hard work and dedication, none of this would be possible. My gratitude to my three amazing sisters—Myla, Elaine and Mary-Anne. Their loving kindness and confidence in me has always made me feel very special.

I would like to thank Lennox Scott, owner of John L. Scott Real Estate, for his leadership and enthusiastic approach to the business of real estate that has been a great source of inspiration over the years. Thanks to Sol Avzaradel and Jim Willner of John L. Scott for their positive and upbeat approach to life and real estate that has been a great encouragement to me. I would also like to thank some of my fellow Realtors who have been good friends and supporters over the years: Tim O'Neil, who originally suggested that I should write this book, and Phillip Rodocker, Carol Walker, Maureen Paszek, and the many other real estate professionals I have had the pleasure of working with over the years.

Sincere thanks to my dear friend Shirley Sels who was my partner in crime for over ten years and who helped me believe in myself and the potential for this book. Her loyalty and devotion are appreciated beyond measure. I have the utmost love and respect for Shirley, her husband, Wally, and their wonderful family.

Heartfelt thanks to all of our clients, many of whom have become good friends, for placing their confidence and trust in us and our real estate team. I thank you for the opportunity to serve you and your ongoing referrals. Our goal is that you remain our customers for life.

And to all my fellow real estate agents out there, and to those who are perhaps considering real estate as a career, I hope you enjoy the book!

—Phil Gerisilo

TABLE OF CONTENTS

SUCCEED IN REAL ESTATE WITHOUT COLD CALLING

INTRODUCTION

This is not a self-help book. It's a story based on Phil Gerisilo's approach to selling residential real estate. We wrote this book in story format for readability, but we left nothing out about how Phil works his business and what his philosophy is.

Phil started out selling real estate on a very part-time basis because he was doing other things in his life. And what started out as his part-time job became his income source for the next fifteen years.

We hope you enjoy the wisdom of the book's message, and if you're pleased with this book, buy several for your struggling friends in your office.

—Rob Lebow

SIX MYTHS OF
REAL ESTATE SALES™

Myth Number One

You won't make any money the first six months in real estate.

Myth Number Two

You have to work very long hours, six and seven days a week.

Myth Number Three

You have to show customers a lot of houses before they can choose one.

Myth Number Four

Open houses are a waste of time.

Myth Number Five

You need to do lots of paperwork to be successful.

Myth Number Six

The Sales Formula—You need lots of fancy training and high-pressure sales techniques to succeed.

SIX GROUND RULES
FOR REAL SUCCESS

*Your answers to these six questions will
establish your personal ground rules for
a truly successful career in real estate.*

1 What is the real value of my service? In other words, what function do I perform? And I'd include my broker's office and franchise in that answer.

2 Am I executing my service in the most straightforward way possible?

3 Am I performing this service with integrity, and am I representing those properties that offer the best long-term value? Am I also resisting the temptation for the shortcuts, quick hits, and too-good-to-be-true sales?

4 Am I addressing the needs of my customers, and can I honestly say that this purchase or sale will be in *their* long-term interests?

5 Is the quality and value of the property understood by the buyer, including location issues, home design, and structural integrity?

6 Have I put the interests of both the buyer and seller before my own?

Chapter One

ONE

The Homecoming

THUMBNAIL: Our beliefs dictate our behaviors and actions. The power and mystery of beliefs are best described as our paradigms.

Paradigms are the unique sets of rules we accept which most often predestine our actions and affect our success. Often, paradigms are invisible.

B*eep ... Beep ... Beep!* The piercing shrill of a 5:30 A.M. wake-up call rudely roused Margaret Williams from the comfort and security of her warm northern New Jersey bed. Mar, as her friends and associates called her, was planning a visit to her parents' home in Texas and needed the early start to catch the 7:15 flight to Houston.

Mar's father worked for a major airline, and she was using one of the family passes to visit her folks.

Mar felt a certain amount of guilt because she was leaving her real estate business at the worst possible time. She knew there was never a good time to leave a business that seemed to run nonstop, 365 days a year. The truth was, subconsciously, she was escaping and needed this time to reorganize her thoughts. For the past several weeks, she'd had recriminations about her decision to leave the security of the teaching world and was having second thoughts about her ability to ever be able to support herself by selling real estate, without dipping into her meager savings.

Mar recognized her time in the business was short compared to many of the real estate agents in her office, and she knew that she would have to pay her dues just like everyone else. So far, she hadn't set the world on fire. Before taking the plunge into the entrepreneurial lifestyle of a real estate agent, Mar had been a tenured high school teacher. The contrast from the safe life of a steady paycheck was taking its toll. Her past life and education seemed a thousand miles away as she finished packing and loaded her dark blue nylon suitcase into her four-door, late-model sedan.

Waiting in the check-in line at the airport these days was a long-term commitment, but it gave Mar time to survey the people around her. She was a people person and loved to watch and analyze them. Her projections and intuitive skills had come from trying to read the faces of her high school kids. This skill was handy in her newly chosen career.

Waiting in line, she became impatient. It was less than 60 minutes to scheduled take-off and the ticket validation/seat selection line was long.

In preparation for her trip, Mar had bought two books on real estate as traveling companions. She hadn't had much time to read for pleasure since she'd left the teaching profession. She missed the time off that teaching had afforded her. Now, she read strictly for business.

Her first book selection covered listing and closing sales in real estate. The second book detailed time management techniques—an important subject that needed her attention because she was always running up against the clock. She never seemed to have the time to do all the many things the experts said you needed to do to be successful.

The book on listing and closing was the fourth book on this subject she had read during the past year and a half. The books were helpful enough, but unfortunately, she'd been unsuccessful in putting their theories into practice. Undaunted, Mar continued to search the bookstores for information on selling real estate because meaningful training at her office was rare. When she did take the time to go to a course, she paid for it out of her own pocket.

Mar's training experiences weren't much different from those of most of her associates. Her formal training consisted of sixty hours of instruction on how to pass the real estate licensing exam. After the franchise broker had selected her, she attended a three-day seminar on basic real estate selling skills. She was on her own after completing the *crash* course. Mar now realized that if she is going to succeed she would need to acquire a few of the finer points. But where could she go to receive this information?

As Mar's flight was called, she moved towards Gate 52 with the other morning travelers. It would be a good, clear day for flying. What Mar didn't realize was, this flight would have a profound affect upon her future in the real estate business.

As the aisle began to clear, several of the flight attendants began counting passengers and shutting overhead compartments. The rhythmic snap of the hinged overhead doors distracted Mar. As she looked up, she saw that her companion for the first leg of the passage to Washington, D.C., was a conservatively dressed businessman in his late fifties. Mar hardly paid attention to the man while he secured his overnight carry-on above her head.

"Hi," said the stranger, half smiling while he buckled his seat belt. "I guess we'll be traveling together to D.C."

Mar thought this stranger's friendly-but-direct manner somewhat intruding. She smiled guardedly and tried to take refuge behind her book—the only weapon she had at hand.

As the plane taxied towards the runway, the man looked at Mar's book. "I see you're interested in real estate?"

Mar smiled as she glanced to her right. "I'm a little more than interested in the subject. I'm a relatively new real estate agent and can use all the help I can get." The

stranger nodded knowingly. Her companion said that he had been in the real estate industry for nearly thirty years, adding that it hadn't all been smooth sailing.

"Commercial or residential?" asked Mar.

"Residential," said the stranger. "By the way, I hope I don't appear to be out of line, but I've found that most of the books you'll read will give you more bad habits and bum steers than you can imagine." The stranger's sparkling eyes suggested that he wasn't trying to insult these writers, but was sincerely convinced that what he had just said *was* true.

Mar's interest had been piqued by the stranger's unusual and provocative comment, so she put her book in her lap and turned towards him. "I'm not sure I understand what you mean. How can reading a book from this leading authority on listing houses and closing sales possibly give me any bad information? After all, this book has sold over a million copies. Can all those readers be wrong?"

Mar's traveling companion had heard this challenge before, so he knew that she was asking a legitimate question that required a sincere answer. "Let me introduce myself. My name's Frank Newman. For the past seven years, I've been teaching real estate agents a *new* approach to selling homes. This approach works for everyone who tries it in their very *first* month in business."

At that, Frank extended his hand and Mar introduced herself. Mar noticed that Frank's handshake and eye contact were the sincerest she had experienced in a long while. His demeanor was open and warm. She thought to herself, no wonder he's been successful.

Frank was all business, if you could ignore the twinkle in his eye. Here was a man, Mar thought, who really enjoyed life. He was a natural teacher, that was pretty obvious from how he couched his comments, and he seemed to exude a quiet confidence as well. Mar's evaluation was interrupted by Frank's answer to her question.

"You have asked two very important questions. First, how can reading books written by leading authorities possibly give you bad information? And second, can all the people who bought the books be wrong?"

Frank paused for the briefest of moments and gently began to weave his answer with the utmost care and skill. "Bad habits and bum steers come from the most well-intentioned people. It's not that anyone maliciously plants false information in our heads, but the effects are the same. Let me see if I can explain.

"Last year tens of thousands of hopeful people entered the residential real estate industry in North America and close to that same number of people left the industry. Do you want to know why they left?" Mar could sense a frustration in Frank's voice.

Mar knew the answer from experience. "Because they didn't make any money!" she said, smiling with satisfaction.

Frank smiled back. "Yes, but I believe that was the *result* and not the cause of *why* they left."

Mar was puzzled. "Wait a minute, what do you mean it wasn't the cause? If the lack of money wasn't the cause, then what was the reason?"

Frank smiled openly, paused, and phrased his answer carefully. "The lack of money was the eventual reason so many of the agents left the business, but it was *not* the cause. The cause was a set of beliefs that no longer work for people. And yet, practically everyone still believes they do.

"Please understand that our beliefs are so powerful that new information and facts have little effect in shaking our convictions about how things *really* work."

"Aren't beliefs changed with new information?" Mar asked quickly, her impatience showing. "Before becoming a real estate agent, I taught school. I was always teaching new ideas. For the most part, these ideas were accepted by my students."

"I think there's a difference," said Frank. "When you taught young people new information, their minds were not already *fixed* on any particular point of view. Try changing their minds in the future by introducing new information and I think you'd see what I mean. We've all heard the expression, 'you can't teach old dogs new tricks.' So let's now address your questions one at a time.

"First, let's discuss the dynamics surrounding beliefs before we talk about the secret that will lead you towards becoming a wildly successful agent. I'd like to talk about the power of paradigms and how they affect our beliefs. Do you know what a paradigm is?" asked Frank gently.

Mar thought for a moment. "Paradigms have something to do with how we think about things, isn't that right?"

Frank nodded. "Yes. *Paradigms define our belief systems.* With these beliefs come a set of rules. They are the boxes in which we tend and guard our garden of attitudes.

They are the boundaries and walls we construct around our convictions and values. In short, the paradigms we hold help form, more than any other single factor, our decisions and reactions, even in the face of facts. Once formed, it literally takes a nuclear bomb to penetrate this invisible wall."

Mar interjected. "What does this have to do with my real estate business? I don't see the connection."

"It has *everything* to do with your real estate business—and the careers of millions of people who share the same invisible real estate paradigms. As you go about your business, you and others re-enforce your beliefs by gathering examples, data points, and other information. But paradigms are invisible, and you don't realize you have them—and that's the frightening aspect of paradigms. Mar, I'd be surprised if those books you have on your lap aren't supporting existing real estate paradigms that no longer work." Mar was transfixed by what she was hearing.

Frank continued. "The most dangerous part about paradigms is that they are invisible and shield us from new information that would alter our decisions, behaviors, and success. Over the years, I've witnessed agents, brokers, and entire organizations with nonfunctioning paradigms so strong that they would rather go out of business than modify their beliefs. You might consider it a form of"—Frank paused briefly—"cutting off your nose to spite your face." Frank looked closely at Mar to make sure she was still following his argument.

He continued. "Let me see if I can give you an example to dramatically bring home the point. Nearly 400 years ago there was a dominant scientific paradigm: *The earth is the center of the universe and all heavenly bodies revolve around it.* Science, history, politics, legends, religion, and Western culture depended on this paradigm.

"Fortunately, not everyone believed this paradigm. It was a young Polish mathematician named Copernicus, one of history's great scientists, who argued on factual grounds that the earth was *not* the center of the universe. As you might suspect, there were many vested interest groups threatened by this mathematically based pronouncement. If Copernicus was right, Western society would be turned topsy-turvy. Religion, politics, and science would be enormously affected—even destroyed. If Copernicus's idea was accepted, literally all beliefs that were built around the existing paradigm—that the earth was the center of the universe—would have to be redefined and their power base disrupted forever. As we know from history, Copernicus was *not* popular and was excommunicated for his pronouncement. To this day, his discovery is still echoing in the corridors of power. Back then, it did not echo ... it *thundered!*"

Mar interrupted. "I don't think you need to go on. I think I've got it. Columbus wouldn't have discovered America, the Wright Brothers would never have built the first heavier-than-air motor-driven airplane, and most women would still not be enjoying the same rights as men, if we hung on to our 'old' paradigms."

"Exactly! I couldn't have said it better myself," said Frank, with some pride. "Imagine all the paradigms that have fallen into rubble in just the past twenty years. The

Berlin Wall, communism itself, and the emergence of Japan as a leading economy, to name but a few."

"And in my father's industry, who would have imagined the number of airlines that have been on the verge of going out of business!" said Mar.

"Yes, our beliefs affect us as individuals, as companies, and even as nations. Take your father's industry for a moment. Many of the airlines were unwilling and unaccepting of new ways to do business, especially after deregulation. In fact, many resisted change so fanatically that they went out of business rather than change their approach. They saw price, and not service, as their success paradigm.

"Most airlines still haven't gotten the message, and they demonstrate this by the way they treat people and their possessions, crowd them into tiny seats, and serve them less than acceptable meals. By separating 'classes' of service, airlines cling to an old paradigm. I would bet

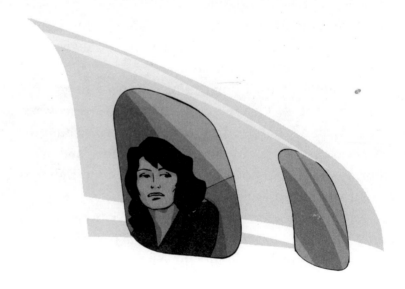

you that if any airline would start with a blank piece of paper and sketch out service that included comfortable seats, prompt check-ins, and safe baggage handling, that airline would *dominate* the industry and establish a new paradigm of service. As you know, I just described Southwest Airlines."

"Boy, it sounds like you've just defined first-class service for *everyone*," said Mar.

"Exactly. *When we treat everyone in a first-class way, we've designed for any industry the blueprint for its success and have established the ultimate competitive advantage.* I believe there are enough people who will respond to the approach of first-class service to make any company that follows this simple prescription a stand-out winner in any industry."

Frank smiled, knowing that his bright companion was open and accepting the possibility that there were paradigms involved in what we believe and how we conduct our business.

Frank continued. "Now that we've established a common understanding of how powerful our beliefs are and how they color our behavior and decisions, I'd like to address your question about what this has to do with our business—residential real estate."

As Frank proceeded, he visibly slowed his pace and paused deliberately. "Now, remember how the people of the 1500s reacted to Copernicus's findings, because I'm about to share with you a new paradigm for the real estate industry—one that is so different from what you're used to believing and experiencing that you'll be tempted to reject it out-of-hand."

At that, Mar encouraged Frank to go on: "Come on, Frank, give me a little more credit than that. I'm a big girl! I can take it. How crazy can it be?"

"All right. Here goes!" Frank drew a deep breath. *"What if I were to tell you that you can make $100,000 your first year in real estate without being a great salesperson or ever having to cold call to create listings?"*

"You're right, Frank. YOU'RE CRAZY AND I'M CHANGING MY SEAT ... *FLIGHT ATTENDANT!* You must be from another planet," said Mar, smiling and joking. "I've been busting my back for the past eighteen months, working six and seven days a week, and I haven't cracked $20,000." At that, both travelers fell silent in seriousness.

Frank had experienced this reaction many times before. He knew that Mar was saying these things in a spirit of disbelief and frustration, but underlying her comments was a genuine yearning to understand how, in heaven's name, his statement could be true.

As Mar finished her comments, the airline's beverage cart pulled up next to them. The attendant leaned towards Row 17, and Mar turned and requested an orange juice without ice. Frank's turn was next. "I'd just like some decaf coffee, please."

The interruption allowed both travelers to reflect upon their positions. Mar broke the ice. "The fact is that I'm working harder than I have ever worked before, and I can't say I'm having a lot of fun *or* a lot of success. Maybe if I made more money at this I'd at least believe all the hard work was worth it."

As Mar spoke, Frank observed that she had become more depressed and he sympathized with her plight.

She continued. "Frankly, your statement about making $100,000 the first year is *crazy*. I know of only one person in my office that makes that kind of money. Everyone else makes a great deal less. And come to think of it, if your information is correct, how come I've not met anyone who has ever suggested that you can be new in real estate sales and make gobs of money?"

Frank listened without portraying any defensiveness. He listened carefully and allowed Mar as much time as she needed to vent her frustrations and disbeliefs. Then, at the appropriate moment, Frank began.

"Mar, remember Copernicus?"

"Yes, I remember our earlier discussion. But I reacted the way I did because your comment goes against everything I believe or have experienced," said Mar, almost apologetically.

"Now you know firsthand why paradigms are so dangerous to and emotional for us mortals." Mar could see that Frank had been on the other end of the paradigm dilemma once or twice before.

Frank continued. "In your heart-of-hearts, you believe your experience and information are correct. Believe me, you're not the first to face the real estate paradigm dilemma. Remember the good people of the sixteenth century? You're not a fool and you have confidence in what you observe and experience. Along comes a complete stranger with a different point of view, and you're not able to accept this new position, *certainly not without some conclusive evidence*. After all, if you were to accept this new paradigm, wouldn't you be admitting that the past eighteen months had been wasted? And how would that make you feel?"

Without knowing it, Frank had hit the nail on the head. If Frank was right, she would have wasted eighteen months. To someone as impatient as Mar, wasting that much time would be a sin. And she would have only herself to blame.

But—if Frank *could* show her "some conclusive evidence" to support his wild claims, then she would listen. After all, she had always prided herself on being open-minded. Mar turned to Frank. "Listen, we've only got about 40 minutes before you get off in D.C. If you have evidence about earning $100,000 a year, starting with your first year in real estate, please tell me as much as you can."

Frank was pleased that Mar was open-minded enough not to dismiss his claims out-of-hand, but he needed to make one more point. "Mar, who said anything about getting off in D.C.? My destination is Houston."

Mar's eyes widened with pleasure because she would have more time to explore Frank's statement. "I assumed that you were getting off in D.C. when you first got into the seat and said, 'We'll be traveling to D.C. together.' "

Frank took Mar's comment as his cue to tell a story. "Mar, it's funny how we project our ideas and reach conclusions without all of the appropriate information. Sometimes it's a dangerous thing to do. I often do that myself, so I'm not being critical. Let me tell you a funny

story that happened several years ago to a friend of mine's sister.

"Nancy Parker is her name. I met her at a workshop I was giving on earning $100,000 a year in real estate. She told me a story that she thought epitomized how our minds sometimes jump to the wrong conclusion.

"That previous fall, Nancy's sister Kate had finally bought the car of her dreams. It was a new, blue convertible with all the options. Kate lived in California in the Del Mar area, just north of San Diego. On weekends, she would often take the opportunity to hop in her convertible early in the morning and drive the curved roads with the top down. Kate liked doing this more than almost anything else.

"Well, as I remember the story, on this one particular Saturday, as Kate was driving on old US 101 around a *blind curve,* the driver in an oncoming car, swerving from lane to lane, screamed out the window at Kate, 'COW!' Kate couldn't believe her ears. Here was this madman, almost hitting her, calling *her* a cow!

"As you can imagine, Kate was pretty darned angry and upset. Just as she entered the last part of the blind curve, Kate realized what this crazy driver was *really* saying. It was a piece of information that she neither expected nor could have imagined. Smack in the middle of the road was a milk cow!

How it got there, no one ever
found out. But it took all of
Kate's skill and agility to steer
around the cow and remain in
control of her beloved new car.
You see, the driver of the other
car was *warning* her ... not *crit-
icizing* her!

"It's funny how our minds
look for information to corrobo-
rate our beliefs. And it's pretty
much the same with the information I'm about to give
you. If you take this new information and put it to use
immediately, you can literally create a revolution in your
real estate earnings.

"For the next hour or so, would you promise me that
you'll try to stop jumping to conclusions based on information you believe to be true? If you will, it will be my
pleasure to share with you six remarkable ideas that are
yours for the taking. *I know these ideas will change
your real estate paradigm as they did mine!*"

Mar concentrated intently on what Frank was saying.

Startled by the flight attendant who placed breakfast
on her tray table, Mar tingled with excitement as she
sensed that her real estate career and the way she conducted business were about to change forever.

Chapter Two

TWO

Throw Out the "Myth Bag"

THUMBNAIL: Our myths blind us to alternative ways of orga-nizing our activities, especially when we don't recognize that they are only myths. Most real estate agencies actually hand out "Myth Bags" to new agents without knowing it, and then they reinforce these myths through their well-intentioned training programs and help sessions.

A s Mar ate her breakfast, she knew that Frank was serious about what he was willing to share with her. She wasn't convinced that she could ever earn that kind of money, and she didn't know what to expect, but she was willing to listen.

She realized she could tell Frank that she wanted to continue to read her real estate book or she could take the chance that Frank knew what he was talking about. Mar decided that the book in her lap could wait.

"Frank, I think I'm ready to listen to the *new* real estate paradigm."

"Great! But before we plunge into that with both feet, I need to cover one more concept. It's what I call "the myths of our business." And like paradigms, myths blind us to alternative thinking. Well-intentioned people hand down myths like paradigms to us.

"Myths seem to be some of the building blocks that make up our paradigms. In other words, myths are allegories that we take for granted. Unlike paradigms, we won't defend them with the same amount of vigor, but nevertheless they are major influencers in our beliefs and our approach to conducting our real estate business. Unless we challenge these myths one by one, they remain part of our belief system, and the basic way we conduct our business won't change."

"Can you give me an example of a real estate myth and the process that arises from believing that myth?" asked Mar.

"You bet. I can give you quite a few. In fact, it's the myths of the business that we'll examine to create the *new* real estate paradigm and the innovative approach that supports it. Once we understand what the myths are, conducting business will be amazingly simple and straightforward.

"Myths come in a large bag," said Frank, quite seriously.

"A Myth Bag," said Mar, catching the rhythm of the idea.

"Exactly," said Frank, smiling with satisfaction.

Frank settled back in his aisle seat and began to examine the first myth. He knew Mar would need to know as much as she could about each myth if she was to cast out her old paradigm and enter into a new world of real estate success.

"I bet you've heard the idea that it takes years to build your business, that you need to be patient before you become successful. We've all heard old-timers talk about 'paying your dues' and how you need to be prepared to starve for the first six months."

MYTH NUMBER ONE: You won't make any money the first six months in real estate.

"That was certainly true for me," said Mar.

"Believe me when I say that you can start earning a good income right from the beginning. Now, the tricky part is that you need to understand the whole series of myths surrounding this old paradigm before you can begin to earn money immediately." Frank's enthusiasm was transparent.

"I think I should stop you," interrupted Mar. "If I understand what you're saying, Frank, I should've explored all the old myths and understood the new paradigm before I started in the business."

"Theoretically, that would be ideal. Realistically, very few people get hold of this information first and then enter the real estate industry. For the majority of us, it's pretty much on-the-job training. For someone like you, who's been in the trenches for awhile, disproving these myths and accepting the new real estate paradigm is all that's necessary to start conducting your business differently *and*, might I add, in a more efficient and less frustrating manner.

"It's a misconception to believe that people come into the real estate business without experience. Living is quite an experience, and I believe it's safe to say that this is our on-the-job training. After all, most businesses are dependent on interpersonal relationships. If you understand this, you'll go a long way in understanding how to satisfy your customers' needs.

"Let's take the myth about not earning any money for six months head-on by exploring the most prevalent aspects."

"Sounds great to me," said Mar intently.

Frank began, "I've known real estate agents, plenty of them, who'll tell you that they literally starved for six months in the business. Frankly, they didn't need to. Granted, it will take you years to build your reputation and market savvy, but that should *not* mean you can't begin to enjoy a substantial income in the first forty-five to sixty days. Let me explain.

"Have you ever had the experience of going the whole day with a particular article of clothing ripped and you didn't know it? You conducted yourself as usual, and the reaction from the people you were conducting business with was normal. Had you known about the rip in your clothes, you would have felt self-conscious or worse, but because you didn't know about it, it didn't affect your composure or actions. Well, it's the same about this first myth. If you buy into the myth, you will act far differently than if you didn't know it existed.

"Let me see if I can add some recent statistics and support what I just said. Less than 10 percent of the customers you work with will ask or care about how long you've been in business. In most cases, they will 'buy' you and trust you because of how you feel about yourself. In this recent survey, people were asked how they selected their agent. The single biggest response was centered upon the agent's behavior and not the length of experience he or she had in the business.

"What this suggests is that your best opportunity to attract customers is not guaranteed by your years of experience but by your behavior, or persona. If you're confident and knowledgeable about the market and available properties, you have as good a chance as any long-term veteran. In fact, the only reason you wouldn't have this confidence is if you're holding on to the myth bag that your broker gave you—that people *buy* experience," added Frank. "For some crazy reason, older realtors will let you know either subtly or in no uncertain terms that 'Kid, you need to pay your dues!' "

"Aren't you being a little hard on brokers when you refer to their handing a myth bag to the new, unsuspecting agent?" asked Mar, with a small smile.

"Yes and no. Yes, because it's placing some blame on the brokers, and no, because the facts speak for themselves. Mar, you may be familiar with this statistic, for it dramatically illustrates my point. On average, the typical residential real estate agent earns $23,000 per year. Now, granted that represents both full- and part-time realtors, but all-in-all, that's not what I'd call a great success story. How about you?" asked Frank.

Mar realized that Frank was talking about her, too. "My first half year wasn't very hot. Come to think of it, the older, more experienced agents warned me on several occasions about the six-month drought. And boy, did my income live up to their predictions!" Both Mar and Frank laughed.

"If you're suggesting that they were handing me one of the classic myths out of the myth bag, then how come so many rookies have a dry first six months?" asked Mar with interest. "I'm not sure I'd characterize these results as being myth related unless you show me proof!"

Frank smiled broadly. "O.K., let me go on. Maybe we should come at this from another direction. When you first entered the business, did anyone counsel you about being patient?"

"Of course they did. They said that it would take years to build my business, that I needed to become committed to this profession, and that I shouldn't become discouraged if things didn't happen overnight," reflected Mar. "How can you imply that those are myths?"

"Because, after I explain a few more of the myths that have to do with skills and strategies, you'll recognize how the myth of taking years to build your business is just that, a myth, and how it's affected your thinking and your expectations," remarked Frank calmly.

"Some brokers believe that their newest agents are the least productive group to work with. So they take a wait-

and-see attitude, and this attitude permeates the relationship the entire office—administrative staff as well as fellow
realtors—has with the new people. Believing that these new
folks won't be around for long, they conclude, 'Why both-
er to become colleagues? Why get involved?' And, in many
cases, they won't even learn the new people's names!"

Mar let this information dance around her head ...
but she knew Frank understood how she'd been feeling
and now she could put a name on it ... prejudice, at least
a form of it.

Frank continued. "Brokers have traditionally seen
high turnover rates in this segment of their office. They
have come to believe that until a new agent is at least six
months in the business, they shouldn't spend much time
with them because it would be a futile investment. They
have encouraged new agents to *cold call* and *knock on
doors* in an effort to list homes to build business."

"What's wrong with that idea? That *is* what I did for
the first six months," said Mar.

"Nothing, if you want to starve!" said Frank. "In fact,
the way we gain buy-in from others into our myths is to
come up with procedures that reinforce the myths. In
this case, we recommend to new people that they perform the hardest activity in our business first!"

"Frank, are you saying that I shouldn't have attempt-
ed to list homes?"

"No, I'm saying the way you were encouraged to go
about building your business is contrary to the facts that
I'll be sharing with you shortly," said Frank.

"Let me ask you a question. If you had *not* spent the
effort cold calling to list houses your first six months,
what would you have spent your time on?" asked Frank.

"That's easy. I would have spent it working with buyers," stated Mar confidently.

"Exactly! You would have spent more time with *buyers,* and in doing that, you'd have experienced a *totally* different level of financial success and personal satisfaction."

"But my broker *encouraged* me to list homes," said Mar.

"Yes, and who gained the major benefit from this activity?"

"It was me ... I think?" Mar's reflection caused her face to scrunch up like a little kid who didn't want to displease her third-grade teacher.

"Mar, with all due respect to your broker, the major benefactor was *not* you but the broker," said Frank, lowering his voice purposefully.

"Listen, I'm not suggesting that you wouldn't have eventually received income from listing a home. What I'm saying is that the strategy of listing homes for a new person right out of the chute is crazy. The turnaround time from listing to selling a multiple listing and receiving the commission is from four to seven months in most American communities.

"Let's say, for this example, that it takes you thirty days of really hard cold calling to get your first listing. In fact, that isn't bad and is the national average for new agents. If you tack on to this the time it takes to sell the average $325,000 home, say, four to five months, and add on to that the closing time of forty-five days ... well, as you can see, enjoying any income for the first six months is no myth, it's simple mathematics.

"The reality is that you could have enjoyed a more predictable and immediate income from selling a home that was *already* listed.

"Mar, in short, *in starting out, new agents should only do those things that equate to immediate income.* If new agents take this approach, they'll break the six-month rookie cycle without any cold calling! I'd venture to say that this is a good rule of thumb to follow.

"One final note on the myth of having to have many years of experience before you enjoy success. Many experienced realtors believe that you have to pay your dues. *Mar, the real estate business doesn't require dues to be paid.*" Frank smiled impishly as he said this. "It requires knowing a certain number of skills, taking appropriate and consistent action, and understanding how things work."

Mar was stunned. How could it be so simple? She was embarrassed to admit to Frank the number of painful hours she had spent knocking on strange doors, calling expired listings, and hunting down dead-ends during her first six months. Imagine, NO COLD CALLING!

"Frank, this is amazing. If you had only told me about this eighteen months ago, my early success rate would have been so different!"

At this point, Frank was animated. "My guarantee to you or to anyone else is this: If you buy into the myth about it taking a long time to build your business, it will!

"And not only that, but it will become part of your personal belief system and you will unknowingly pass it on like the flu to someone else. You'll be programmed to fail or, at the very least, to participate in many time-wasting activities. As an equally dangerous side note, you will, *out of kindness,* pass this myth along to the next class of rookies," cautioned Frank.

Mar had fallen completely silent.

Overhead, the captain's voice announced that the plane would be landing in Washington, D.C., in the next several minutes. As the flight attendants made their final check of the passenger cabin, Mar turned to Frank. "It seems as though I've been going about this business all wrong."

"Don't be so hard on yourself. I believe you've probably done many things right," said Frank, consoling Mar.

As the plane made its final descent and the wheels touched down, Mar knew that her real education had just begun.

Chapter Three

THREE

Make Time Work for You

THUMBNAIL: *Everyone agrees that time is a precious commodity. Taking the time to listen to people means that you must become more interested in what others have to say than in what you want to tell them.*

"Well, what do you say about stretching our legs? We have about forty minutes before we take off again," said Frank.

"That sounds like a great idea to me," said Mar.

As they walked into the gate area, Mar couldn't wait to ask her next question.

"Frank, you spoke about time-wasting activities, but I'm more interested in the activities that really help one make money."

"Mar, that's a great attitude to have. But let's not forget about our myth bag. It still plays a pretty big part in how we behave and perform."

> **MYTH NUMBER TWO: You have to work very long hours, six and seven days a week.**

Frank studied Mar carefully as they walked. "Mar, I'm always reluctant to give someone else advice. Maybe it's because advice almost always seems to appear easily gathered. After all, how can a word or two from another person be profound when it comes from someone other than a great thinker or from a classic book? But ignoring my own counsel, I do have an opinion on how many of us waste time.

"You've heard all the clichés about time. Many of them are true. I believe I can put a twist on how you might think about time: Time is a precious commodity, one that has an integrity all its own. Respect its value and others will respect your time. Freely give it to those who deserve it. Guard it jealously from those who regard it with little value.

"The best way to guard your time is to observe how others think and behave. Listen to their comments. A wise man once told me that in every remark is a *request*.

Meet that request and you will build trust, fulfill the hidden needs of customers, and enjoy riches far beyond the common experience."

As they walked on, Frank related an incident that had occurred many years ago. "While I was first knocking around in real estate, not really knowing or recognizing how to conduct my business with the consistency that I now have, I met one of the richest men in America. And without knowing it at the time, I learned a lesson I'll never forget.

"I was introduced to this man through a friend in one of the local service organizations in Minneapolis. Frankly, you would not have picked this man to be particularly wealthy. Nothing about him was distinguished or uncommon. His only unusual quality was his unbridled enthusiasm."

"What do you mean, 'unbridled enthusiasm'?" asked Mar.

"It was unbridled in the sense that it was overwhelming in its intensity. There was a certain sparkle, an almost childlike quality to it. The man was neither loud nor imposing. On the contrary, he was modest and almost quiet. Yet his gaze and brief comments encouraged you at every turn. His enthusiasm for other's remarks was extraordinary, and his acceptance of those around him was noteworthy. I remember distinctly how interested he was in what I had to say. He encouraged me to talk about myself and commended me for it by the words he used and the attention he paid. In a few brief moments, we became friends.

"It wasn't until later that I was told who he was. Here was a man who could have literally bought and sold me a thousand times over. Would I have bought real estate from this man? You bet. And why? Because he listened to me, responded to my questions, and discovered my eagerness to learn more."

As they strolled through the terminal, Mar observed that Frank still retained a youthful spring in his walk, even though he seemed to have amassed much of the wisdom of the ages.

"Mar, buying a home is a major step for people and probably the most important financial decision most families are going to make in their lifetime. Because of this, I've always treated the purchasing of a home with that level of importance. Consequently, I've always been more interested in listening to what *my customer* has to say than in what *I* want to say. In fact, I listen carefully to their hopes, desires, *and* needs."

"How do you become a good listener?" asked Mar.

"It's not easy, but with conscious effort and practice, you can increase your listening skills dramatically. And as we have already discussed, being a good listener is basic to your success as a real estate agent. The first thing we need to do is direct the focus of the conversation away from ourselves and onto the customer. An effective real estate agent encourages the customer to do most of the talking. The agent can help the conversation along by asking questions, but it is most important to allow the customer ample time to consider the question and respond.

"Being a good listener requires patience. It's easy, as agents, to become excited in a selling situation. In an effort to dazzle the customer with our knowledge and insight, we tend to think about what we're going to say next, rather than listen to what our customer has just said to us. Don't get me wrong, I believe that enthusiasm is a powerful force in selling—we just need to remember to be enthusiastic about what the customer is saying as well.

"People seem to open up more when they feel comfortable with the person they're talking to. I make a point of not jumping right into the topic of real estate when I meet a new prospect. In fact, I would generally prefer to talk about almost anything else first. Try to find a subject that may appeal to your customer. When greeting visitors at an open house, for example, take the time to welcome them and thank them for coming. You might ask them if they own a home in the neighborhood or if they are new to the area. A simple comment regarding the weather or perhaps a recent event might be enough to get a conversation going. I like to try to emulate the conversational style of the customer. If they tend to be quiet or soft-spoken, I tone down my approach. The most important thing to remember is simply to be nice to people and give them every opportunity to talk. Once you have them talking, remember to listen closely for their hidden request. Oh, and one more thing—acceptance of others, and not prejudging, is essential.

"When people are looking for a home, it's usually an emotionally charged time for them. Yet most people try to approach the buying process logically. You're talking big dollars: what will fit their needs financially and what will suit their lifestyle. At the same time, nobody wants to buy a house that doesn't appeal to them, to their inner self and needs. You must recognize the strong emotional attachment in every purchase. When someone walks into the *right* home, they usually know it immediately. And when they walk into the *wrong* house, they sense that as well. And if you're looking at them and how their eyes and body react to the house, their response normally gives you a wonderful clue to their preferences.

"They can look at a dozen four-bedroom homes, but only one of the homes is going to be the right home for them. Mar, the next time you're showing houses, look at how their body posture changes from house to house. *They're going to express an emotional attachment for one home more than for any other.* If you're careful to listen to and observe their inner desires, you'll create a shortcut to their decision and help them reach a positive conclusion," said Frank. "If you meet their hopes, desires, and needs, you'll be successful and serve them well in the process.

"Sometimes, as surprising as it might seem, it's not what they're telling you logically that's the deciding factor in their decision, but rather it comes in bits and pieces over the course of the conversation. Sometimes it's the intangibles, such as the brightness of the home, it's curb appeal, how it's situated on the lot, or a feeling of spaciousness. It's only through *listening* that you will key into your customer's true hopes, desires, and needs. Sometimes, we limit our chance for success by jumping to conclusions too early."

Frank paused to make sure that Mar was following him.

"Let me give you an example that taught me another important lesson. When I first began to realize *how* to best serve my clients, I began volunteering for open houses. In the beginning, I did this because I was a little shy and didn't have many chances to meet prospects. Frankly, I thought this was a great way to meet people long before I actually understood how powerful this approach was."

Mar seemed surprised. "You volunteered? Why would you have wasted your time at an open house? I thought you'd be guarding and investing your time wisely, and not wasting it on Looky-Lous."

"Mar, in a few minutes I'll expand my opinion of open houses and their importance, but to continue my story ...

"So, the open house began at 10:00 A.M. I was somewhat skeptical, just like you, that an open house was a productive place to be, because more experienced realtors had warned me against wasting my time, but never-

theless, I was there. And I was *determined* to make the best of it.

"As I recall, there wasn't much traffic in this home until almost twelve o'clock, when in walked a couple in their fifties. He was a pleasant-looking man and his wife, as I remember it, had a very pained expression on her face."

Mar laughed in amusement at Frank's description of an oh-too-frequent event, where one of the house-hunting partners was not there willingly.

Frank continued. "And I interpreted her expression to say that she was there only because her husband had insisted on her being there. He had a strong personality and seemed to get his way more often than not.

"I tried to strike up a conversation with them. The wife wouldn't have anything to do with me. The man was more willing to talk, even though he was guarded and somewhat gruff. I asked a few questions first, trying to be helpful, but to no avail. During the brief conversation, the man told me that they were not *really* in the market for a home and had come to the open house *just* to look. In fact, they had recently leased a home for six months. The man also said he believed that prices and interest rates were sure to improve in the near future, so he wasn't in any hurry to buy.

"Now, those comments would probably serve to discourage the most enthusiastic agent, wouldn't you say, Mar?"

"I would probably have written them off right then and there," replied Mar.

"You and most other agents," Frank confirmed with a smile and a wink, "but let me continue. The man went on to say that he totally disliked the house in which he was standing because it was 'too chopped up.' Through my conversation with him, I learned that he was looking for a home that had an open and airy feeling, preferably a rambler, with a spacious yard. I told them I would be in touch with them, and they left.

"Two days later, I called them on the telephone. In my conversation, I told them I had discovered an exciting home I truly believed they would want to see. This enthusiastic approach broke the ice and created some curiosity. I suggested that we meet on Saturday morning. The home was a contemporary split-level. Even though it wasn't a rambler, I was sure this was really what the husband was describing because of the large number of windows and skylights in the house and the bright feeling it portrayed. In addition, the lot provided an open feeling to the home.

"In trying to meet this couple's requirements, I had previewed properties in my market area. I had done my homework, and this couple, I believe, appreciated my efforts. Because of this, they trusted my judgment and took the time to see the home.

"Remember, the wife was not especially happy about accompanying her husband a week earlier, but because of the conversation and the efforts I had made, I believe she opened up to the idea of viewing a home. They agreed to meet me on Saturday morning, and I showed them this contemporary home, the one I believed they would really like, along with two other fine properties.

"The man had spoken about a rambler, and I felt that he especially should see whether that was indeed what he wanted. Additionally, just to make sure that he or his wife had no preference for a two-story, I showed them a two-story as well. They loved the contemporary home, especially the wife, as I expected them to, and bought it that same day. That was my first sale, my very first week in the business!

"To this day, that gruff man and his wife still keep in touch. Over the years, they've referred many customers to me because of their appreciation of my finding the perfect home for them and because it was the first time, they said, an agent had *really listened* to what they were saying."

"I think I understand these points, although I probably try to sell and tell too much and not listen enough," reflexed Mar. "But where is the myth in all this?"

"Mar, this myth is just as bogus as the first one. **Myth Number Two,** *that you have to work really long hours to be successful,* is a lot of nonsense. No one in real estate has ever received a gold star because they've put in 365 perfect days of attendance. In fact, the only award you'll get for putting in those kinds of hours is an award from your local grade school or Rotary Club. You are not rewarded by the *number* of hours you spend, but by what you put *into* your hours."

"I think I've figured out how this myth relates to listening," said Mar. "If you're able to understand the hopes, desires, and needs of customers and meet their emotional issues as well, then you'll be successful in selling them the homes of their dreams."

"You're right," said Frank. "But, there is much more to the myth. Not only do you need to clearly focus on your customers' needs, but you also need to recognize your needs as well. I'm talking about your lifestyle, your family, and your personal life.

"It is critical that you make time for yourself. You need to be able to recharge your batteries on a regular

basis. I'd like to have a dollar for every real estate agent that burns out of the business needlessly.

"Mar, if you buy into the yth that you need to burn the work-candle at both ends, you'll wind up over-stressed and with medical problems," said Frank.

"But many of the people work only part time in our business," said Mar.

"Yes, they do. But they don't work the business in most cases much differently than the full-timers. Mar, whether you're full time or part time, you need to care-fully plan your schedule. Your time is the only invest-ment asset you have. Invest wisely and you'll leverage and multiply your efforts; invest imprudently and you'll squander your assets and become frustrated."

This conversation with Frank underscored to Mar that time *was* her most important asset. Finally, she could attach meaning to something that in the past had only been a cliché.

As these two passengers walked together, they were oblivious to the crowds around them in the D.C. airport.

Chapter Four

FOUR

Serving Your Customers Better, Not Longer

THUMBNAIL: *We often confuse our* service *role with our* sales *role. Outstanding service requires fulfilling the hopes, desires, and needs of our customers. These three opportunities must* not *be measured in the amount of time we spend or the dollars we earn, but in the* quality *of our contribution.*

Frank stopped by one of the many stores in the mall area of the D.C. terminal and bought the morning paper. Scanning the headlines, he commented on the world situation and Congress's latest vote. Turning to Mar, he said, "It's kind of amazing the number of interest groups focused on their own interests and not on America's. I really believe the real estate business needs to be different."

"What do you mean?" asked Mar.

"I guess this relates back to the myth that we are discussing and hopefully dispelling. It's my contention that if you're going to run a successful business in real estate, you must care about your customer's welfare and happiness *way* ahead of your own. When you look at your customers, you can't see them with dollar signs over their heads. That attitude will get you nowhere fast.

"The best agents always take the approach of embarking upon an *adventure* with a customer," said Frank. "If your primary purpose is to make money and *not* to serve others, you'll never reach your full potential. *Entering the business with making money as your primary objective will hold you back.*

"I believe the adventure comes when you truthfully look forward to *serving* others: informing them, protecting them, and helping them clarify what it is that *they* want. Once they feel good about your intentions, you'll feel good about the results and the money will come— lots of it. It seems to always work that way."

Mar knew exactly what Frank meant. "You know, Frank, for a minute I thought you were talking about the teaching profession and not real estate."

Mar went on. "I went into teaching originally believing that I could make a difference in service to others. After a while, this ideal became fuzzy. It got to the point where I began questioning who I was, my goals and my personal values. I went into real estate sales to earn a good income and to build a career. That's not the same reason I went into teaching."

Frank jumped on Mar's observation. "It's interesting that you compared my definition of service to teaching. I'd go one step further and give it another name—*mentoring*. Mentoring is a very special form of teaching. It's the art of teaching and befriending. It's giving a darn about the other guy and committing to a set of fundamental principles."

"I'm not sure I've observed the kind of service you're speaking about very often in my agency," said Mar. "And

I don't honestly believe that the majority of my peers are concerned with being involved by mentoring others in the way you're describing, even though I believe they are honest and sincere. I think there's a *big* difference, just as you said."

"Mar, you've picked up on a very subtle but *important* point. Most real estate people would define service in terms of how well we follow up, our professional skill levels, and our ability to be knowledgeable about the market, financing parameters—the list could go on."

Mar encapsulated Frank's point. "So, what you're driving at—and what I'm really glad you believe in—is 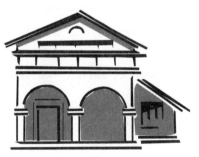 the *joy of serving others.* In other words, get involved in an egoless and selfless relationship. To put it in my dad's old Yankee terminology, 'Look out for the other guy!'"

"Exactly! You probably know that you can't train to it and you can't fake it. But if you possess this feeling, your success opportunities go sky high," summarized Frank.

Frank was pleased with his companion's self-realization and intuitive grasp of this fundamental human issue.

"I'd like to make one more brief comment. It seems as though a sales career, especially one in real estate sales, brings us very close to the precipice separating our personal interests and our customers' interests. I call this the *integrity dilemma,* or *our moment of truth.*

"For each of us, we ultimately need to look in the mirror and decide why we're in sales. Putting the interests of others before our own is mutually beneficial, and the choice is always a personal one to make.

"If our motivation is primarily money and not the joy of serving others, then eventually, we'll come to despise our jobs, our career, and lastly, ourselves."

Frank turned and looked at his watch, conscious of the fact that he was getting pretty serious with Mar. "Well, it's almost quarter to nine. We should get back to the plane. I believe they'll be reboarding soon."

Mar nodded in agreement as they headed towards their gate.

Even though they walked in silence, their last comments somehow bonded these two people in a way that Mar hadn't experienced since her days in the Peace Corps. Maybe it was the purpose and vision of their discussion

that had so excited her, but she knew that this trip to Houston would be remembered for a long time. As they entered the plane, Mar noted that this leg of her journey would be less crowded and she was glad of that.

They buckled up and readied themselves for the two-and-a-half-hour trip. Mar couldn't help feeling how lucky she was to have met Frank, but she suddenly became aware that she might be intruding on Frank's time.

"Frank, it seems as though we still have a fair amount of myth debunking to do before we land in Houston. Are you sure it's all right if we continue? Maybe I should just sign up for one of your famous workshops."

Frank was touched by Mar's sensitivity and graciousness. "Well, I'd love for you to do that at a later date. But thank you for your concern. Believe it or not, I do enjoy sharing this information. After all, I am saving you from the fate of reading about an old real estate paradigm."

Mar laughed and Frank smiled.

Frank went on. "Let's see. Where were we? Oh, yes, the integrity dilemma between our need for sales and our purpose to serve.

"A few moments ago, I promised I would expand on my statement about quality time. In it, I tried to be careful how I defined time. My statement centers on taking the time to listen to people, while guarding against becoming too interested in what *you* want to say.

"So far, this idea is not complete until we add the missing ingredient—*value*. As simple as it might seem, value seems to be left out of many customer/agent relationships."

To drive his point home, Frank asked, "What is value? I believe *value* emanates from how well we match the *home's* value to the hopes, desires, and needs of the buyer. A high value home strongly complements the buyer's interest," said Frank emphatically.

"So where is the myth in this one?" asked Mar, relishing the question and looking forward to the answer.

"Mar, what is the greatest time consumer and potential time waster in our business?"

"Well, I think I would have to answer that it's driving people around and around looking for the right house," said Mar.

"Why do you drive them around and around?" asked Frank, taking a particular delight in the picture of Mar endlessly driving around faceless customers.

"Because *that's my job*. It is through this process that I'm able to show people the available homes in their price range. Look, Frank, I do know a thing or two. I don't just aimlessly drive people around and around. I think I do a good job targeting their hopes, desires, and needs."

At this point in the discussion, Mar realized that she had become defensive. Maybe it was the phrase "around and around" that had set her off, but he had definitely found one of her "hot buttons."

"Now, don't shoot the messenger on this next question, because it will be my last before I share with you the next myth. What would you say is the typical number of homes you show a buyer?"

Mar was now back in control of her impatience and was ready for the next left hook that Frank seemed to good-naturedly throw at her. She knew Frank was setting her up, but she couldn't figure out where the loophole was, so she answered her friendly inquisitor as truthfully as she could.

"Frank, if this is one of your trick questions, I might take a swing at you with my old-paradigm book!"

"No, I swear, this isn't a trick question," replied Frank, crossing his chest and reflexively covering his face.

"O.K.," said Mar cautiously. "Now, to respond your question, I'll need to explain my answer. As you know, every prospective customer requires a different approach. Some buyers want to see only a few houses, say five to seven, while others may take three or four full days of cruising around before they nail down their top two or three selections."

Myth Number Three: You have to show customers a lot of houses before they can choose one.

As Mar stopped talking, she looked into Frank's eyes to assess his reaction to her carefully crafted answer. She was glad she wasn't playing to an inside straight because she was unable to receive a clue from Frank's expression.

What she heard next astonished her. Had she *not* been buckled up, she might have fallen out of her seat.

"Thank you for your answer. As you suspected,

your answer is the next real estate myth. In fact, it's the single biggest time waster in our business. Once you dispel this one, you'll be surprised at the results.

"**The third myth is that** *you have to show customers a lot of houses before they can choose one.* Now, I'd like to counter this myth with the following simple idea: *'Serve people better, not longer.'* What this means is, in order to serve better and not longer …

"YOU NEED TO SHOW PEOPLE NO MORE THAN *THREE* HOUSES!"

Mar's reaction was swift! "Frank, if I hadn't been with you these past two hours, I'd think you were drinking. How in heaven's name do you expect me to believe this? Only *three* houses, you have to be joking!"

"I know this is pretty hard to believe," said Frank. "Remember, this is a myth we're trying to explode and it's attached to a very well-established paradigm—one of the hardest elements to change in all the world."

"Frank, every fiber in my being tells me that I'd starve and so would the rest of my colleagues in my office if I followed your advice! How can we all be so wrong?" asked Mar in total resignation.

Frank welcomed Mar's question. A reaction like this was familiar to him from years of stating his contrary opinion. "Here is how it works. And it's as simple as the first two myths we've exploded.

"First, you should know your housing inventory. By previewing houses on a regular basis, you'll be able to match customers to the right homes. Let's say you've just said hello to your new buyers. As they sit down, you make them comfortable. Next, you begin to hold a relaxed conversation. Your line of questions centers around their hopes, desires, and needs. You take notes and ask questions to further clarify their comments.

"Now remember, they'll try to be as logical as they can possibly be. Yet there still will be a great many hidden emotional issues that you'll need to uncover if you're to meet and fulfill their hopes, desires, and needs.

"But before we talk about the emotional issues, remember that you'll need to get the financial capabilities and parameters out of the way. Your new customers may have the greatest intentions in the world. But if they don't have the means to afford their hopes, desires, and needs, you're only adding to their personal frustrations and wasting gobs of time. So, their ability to qualify for a mortgage is key!

"And the whole mortgage business is reinventing itself every several years, so you'll need to stay current with the latest financing options ... and boy, are there a lot." Mar smiled, realizing that Frank was just hitting the highlights on the financing topic ... or jungle, as many of her peers called it.

At that, Frank stopped to make sure that Mar was tracking his line of thought. "How are we doing so far?" As he suspected, she was indeed.

"Just great. Please, go on," responded Mar.

"O.K. From experience, I'd suggest you work financial qualifications this way: *Establish a prior relationship with an existing banker or mortgage broker.* Here is the key—your relationship with them is pretty simple. They *must* be committed to serving your customer when *you* choose to work. At this point, you're merely using them to qualify the buyer. Under no circumstance are your customers obligated to use this lender, and you need to make this clear to them. If you decide that you only want to work Saturday, Sunday, and Wednesday, then your financial partner must be available during those days.

"With the advent of electronic voice-mail and paging systems, your lender is always just a phone call away. Ask the top agents in your office who they work with, and you're sure to receive the names of several good lenders in your market area.

"It is literally ridiculous to go one step beyond this point until you have your customer's financial parameters established at your office. If your buyers are uncomfortable with talking to your mortgage contact, then suggest to them that you would be delighted to set up another date to meet in your office when they have a qualifying letter from their chosen lender in hand. In most cases, they will defer to your suggestion.

"As your conversation with them continues, the dynamics of the relationship become more apparent. You'll look for the one individual of the two who 'wears the pants in the family' ... so to speak."

Mar smiled at this image and Frank went on. "You'll continue to listen for the intangibles, such as the physical lightness of the home, new or previously owned, location, schools, number of garage spaces, special features, special interests or hobbies, and the like, nothing really new to you yet."

Frank paused, then continued. "Next, you'll begin to formulate a mosaic in your mind as to what your buyers really want. By the way, in almost all situations, working with only one of the decision-makers will be a great waste of time. In most cases, you'll have to retrace your steps once they're united in search of *their* dream home, so resist the temptation to break this commonsense rule.

"And note, too, I keep referring to your buyer's new *home* and **not** new *house*. The difference in meaning between these two words is fundamental in your ability to meet their hopes, desires, and needs.

"'House' is an impersonal image, while 'home' conjures up warmth, emotion, and fundamental human fulfillment. *Words trigger pictures, and pictures trigger emotions. And it is our emotions that trigger our actions.*

"O.K. You're now ready to begin showing your buyers listing photographs of homes that substantially reflect what they have logically stated. The new concept of "virtual touring" on the Internet should save you and your buyer gobs of time and gas. By showing your clients homes that they say they're in the market for, you've opened up the next level in your conversation. This tests their hopes, desires, and needs one step farther. As they respond to your introduction of each home, you're gathering an ever-clearer picture of what they want. And you're getting closer to their *emotional triggers!*

"Now you're at a critical stage in your service to them. Garnered from your conversation, you should have a sense about what type of home they would truly enjoy owning and coming home to every night. This intuitive leap comes from the past thirty to forty minutes you've spent clarifying their desires once they are financially qualified."

Mar broke in. "Frank, so you're stating that the *emotional trigger* is reached at this point."

"Well, yes and no, Mar. This is, as you say, a critical point, but this is only the first critical point. The next critical point is the *curb appeal* and the *front-door experience* your buyers will feel."

"O.K., Frank, I think I'm seeing the picture you're creating in my mind. But is there more?"

"Yes, there is … a few more details. It's important that you show your customer only homes you have personally previewed. *This means that you must do your homework!* Many sales people think that they can 'roll the dice' at this point and 'pop in' to an unpreviewed home. *And* I bring to your attention one of the cardinal sins in the practice of law which parallels the practice of selling real estate."

Mar interrupted, smiling. "Frank, don't tell me. I think you're saying that a trial lawyer never asks a witness a question he doesn't know the answer to!"

Frank laughed. "That is exactly the point. So you get the meaning as to why you never take the risk of walking into an unpreviewed house—great!

"Before you make the final selection of the three homes you'll show your customer in the field—which let me stress again you've personally previewed beforehand—you have one more piece of business to conduct.

"In any case, I wouldn't reveal the three homes you will show your buyers until the missing financial piece of the puzzle is in hand. You could be far off from what they can afford, and this decision is too important to squander on an educated guess. By holding fast to your process of first securing the financing piece, you are establishing a trust level with them. Going wobbly-legged on this point will almost always welcome surprises, frustrations, and heartaches for your buyer, for the seller, and for you and your broker."

"What if they don't want to use my mortgage contact? They might never come back," asked Mar. "Isn't it better to show them a few houses and then meet with them after they've received a mortgage commitment? You know, build a bond with them."

"Mar, the only way I'd go any further with a buyer is when I know the mortgage size and down payment they can swing. Otherwise, you're shooting in the dark and wasting everyone's time."

"O.K., if they feel comfortable talking to my lender, what happens next?" asked Mar.

"Simple, you go to the next step. And here it is. From your knowledge of or from previewing twelve to eighteen homes in the multiple listing database that synchs with your buyer's pricing range and choice area, you'll select *three* homes that you believe will best meet the buyer's hopes, desires, and needs. The key concept is that you are addressing ultimate *value* with your buyer."

Mar looked somewhat puzzled at Frank's last concept.

Frank saw the puzzled expression on Mar's face. "Please understand that *value* is not merely a *financial* concept, but an *emotional* one. Value has two masters and both must be met." Frank paused to make sure that his bright companion understood the meaning of this crucial concept.

Frank's words were words of caution. *"Only three homes are shown. That is the rule. Break this rule and you will no longer be dispelling the myth and the old paradigm, but buying back into it."*

"Frank, what happens if you get buyers who are also locked into the old paradigm and the old myth? What if they are accustomed to going days and days, dragging through homes to find their dream house?" Correcting herself in time, she said, "I mean, dream *home."*

Frank smiled. "Here's what you do. If your buyers don't find what they're looking for, YOU MUST LET THEM GO!" Frank paused to see Mar's reaction.

"What do you mean, LET THEM GO?"

"Simply that," said Frank. "As nicely as you can, you must explain to them that you could continue to show them *houses,* but that what you have just done is show them three *homes* that you believe they would be happy owning—three homes that meet their hopes, desires, and needs and represent a great value."

"Frank, does it really work that simply?" Mar's tone of voice revealed her disbelief.

"Yes, it does and here's why. First, let's take your existing mind-set. Under the old myth, an agent gives way to brute exposure. The mentality is a numbers game, one that goes something like this: Throw lots of buyers and houses at each other and hope something sticks!

"Mar, that approach works about as well as stabbing in the water to catch a fish with a spear. The tricky part of spearfishing comes back to our paradigm dilemma.

"Remember, paradigms are invisible. We don't know we have them. If everyone in the group, high achievers and poor performers, all behave the same way about this hypothetical fish spearing ritual, you won't question it. Why would you? Everyone seems to concentrate on how well they spear fish and never focuses on the sanity of the process. In fact, most of the conversations center on the length of the spear, the skills associated with throwing the spear—and *not* on the activity or process itself. After all, that's not in question. In fact, if this activity and skill become gender related, such as *real men spearfish*, just try to introduce net fishing as a women's activity to these men.

"In short, the focus centers around differences between the successful fisherman's techniques and tools and the unsuccessful fisherman's lack of success. Sadly, the process itself is *never* questioned, especially from the perspective of serving their best interests. After a while, books are written on the subject and seminars are created that ensure that millions of people will buy into the ritual and false process. *It has now become a way of thinking.*"

"You mean it has become a paradigm," said Mar.

"Exactly!" said Frank. "So whether it's spearfishing or showing multiple houses, the concept and truths behind the false beliefs are pretty much the same."

Mar smiled as she was beginning to get the point that Frank was making. "The game itself begins to take on a life of its own, doesn't it, Frank?"

Frank continued, knowing that Mar understood his analogy. "In support of this opportunity for a paradigm shift, let me tell you about something I just read that's pretty interesting. One of the leading authorities on world-class quality was reported to have remarked that we don't fully understand quality until we measure it against what the customer wants. In the old days, manufacturers dictated the quality criteria, not the customer. In fact, the customer was *never* consulted. Let me see if I can explain why this relates so well to *any* ritual, including spearfishing and dragging buyers around to view multiple houses.

"If the *only* approach or paradigm offered in selling or buying houses is our archaic ritual of dragging hapless customers blindly from house to house, then all agents will measure success by the number of houses they sell *using* this process. They will not concern themselves with their or their buyer's valuable time, nor will they question the process itself. Then along comes a different method or paradigm that *doesn't* require brute force or massive exposure or anything associated with a numbers game as we know it, and it's rejected out-of-hand as *crazy*.

"Ignore the fact that it happens to be five times as efficient as the best brute-force technique, and you begin to understand the contrast and conflicts between the two philosophies.

"Mar, please appreciate that any change threatens not only fishermen, but the spearfishermen's association that has set up a series of beliefs and support structures surrounding their proven, time-honored, blind fishing ritual.

"Spearfishing rests on a pretty old paradigm and so does showing massive numbers of houses to buyers. For

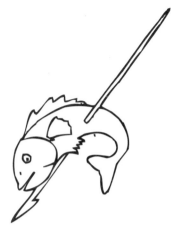

most of us, we would be better served in protecting our customer's interest if we embraced the new approach. Yes, indeed, show only three homes and no more." At that, Frank briefly fell silent and waited for Mar's reaction before continuing.

"Mar, the key to grabbing hold of this myth exploder is a leap of faith, because every book written and every seminar in America today is teaching you better ways to 'spearfish.' Many *experts* discuss the issue as though it's a skill issue, or a fishing issue, when in reality they are focusing on a myth. It is plain crazy!

"It's crazy because it wastes at least ten days out of every month and crazy because the predictability of this existing ritual is by its very nature unpredictable.

"Once you've broken away from the brute-force approach to selling homes, this old-style ritual will appear crazy and any technique that supports the old approach will be politely by-passed.

"In summary, your goal should always be to serve your customers *better,* not *longer.* I believe that using a brute-force approach to selling homes serves neither your buyer nor you and your broker as effectively as disciplining the process and exploding this myth once and for all."

Frank lowered his voice to almost a whisper. "We must do our preliminary homework better to serve better. We must learn to see with our eyes and listen with our ears. We must be interested in what our customers want and need, rather than be drawn to what we want and need. We need to become a servant of our clients' interests; then, and only then, will we feel comfortable showing only a few carefully chosen homes, not a slew of near misses. This is where your ability to read people and fulfill their needs is so important."

"Bravo! I love the images you've painted," said Mar. "Unfortunately, I have one question that begs to be answered, and it's a little way away from our current topic, but I need to ask it," said Mar with respect.

Mar continued with her thoughts. "Doesn't it become more important than ever, then, to be able to prospect and list homes?"

"Prospecting and listing homes has its own set of myths, and this is exactly the right time to discuss them," answered Frank.

Mar was beginning to understand how these myths were interdependent on each other. In addition, she was also accepting Frank's proposition that the new para-

digm was dependent on exploding the series of myths that gives credibility to the old paradigm.

This new philosophy that Frank was outlining made sense, especially in light of the fact that the existing traditions, rituals, and beliefs she had embraced over the past eighteen months weren't working for her, nor were they working very well for most of her new colleagues.

Just then, the beverage and food cart was beside them once again ...

Chapter Five

FIVE

A New Prospecting and Listing Strategy

THUMBNAIL: *Our greatest source for leads has always been the place that is most overlooked*—the open house.

As they began to drink their coffee, Frank started talking about prospecting and listing myths. "It has always amazed me that new people in the real estate business would rather cold call and knock on doors than do the one activity that would get them in front of naturally prequalified prospects."

Mar interrupted. "Excuse me, Frank, but I'm not sure I know the one activity that would get me in front of these natural prospects."

Frank's smile acknowledged Mar's question. "That's an important detail, isn't it, and it's the Fourth Myth. Mar, it's the one undisputed place that is always teaming with prospects—*the open house.*"

"THE OPEN HOUSE!" Mar had to stop herself from

75

choking. "You get more action in a bowling alley, Frank!"

Frank's chuckle could be heard three rows in front and behind them. Collecting himself, Frank inquired, "Why do you say that, Mar?"

"Listen, I worked a couple of open houses, and I didn't enjoy any results for the trouble."

Frank took care with his next point. "Let me see if I can paint a picture for you of why open houses are your gold mine—of course, that is, if you know what to look for.

"Mar, open houses are populated by people who are present and future prospects for home ownership. Once you acknowledge this, you have embraced a new concept and have exploded the fourth myth that states, *open houses are a waste of time.* In fact, open houses are a great source, if not the *best* source, for leads and listings.

MYTH NUMBER FOUR:
Open houses are a waste of time.

"Think of it this way. Granted, many of the lookers are not ready to buy a home and are only there out of curiosity. But not only will these people someday be buyers for new homes, they'll also need to sell their existing homes. Therefore, you have both dynamics—*listing and buying.*

"Mar, I don't know of a better place for a new or experienced agent to be than at an open house. I've come to appreciate the fact that this is our playing field. And it requires our finest hour. All the fixings for the *feast* are there. Here's my list of ingredients:

- The people who have self-selected themselves by being there in the first place,
- Your product which helps define the criteria for the prospect's hopes, desires, and needs, and
- The capable real estate agent who is prepared to connect the buyer with the seller.

"Open house visitors epitomize one of the best examples of a captive audience that I can imagine. Yet most agents don't see them as a golden opportunity at all."

At that, Frank took his pen and listed three important points on his napkin. Then he drew the outline of a house around his points.

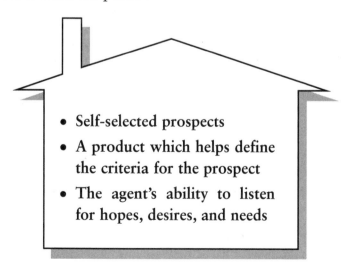

- Self-selected prospects
- A product which helps define the criteria for the prospect
- The agent's ability to listen for hopes, desires, and needs

Frank looked directly at Mar as he continued. "Because of this, many of the best prospectors are *quiet* about this veritable diamond field—and why wouldn't they be? Over the years, I've acquired a pretty effective approach to speaking with people in this situation, along with a very healthy respect for the power of the open house.

"Here's how it works. The first thing you need to know is that most listing agents find it a drag running open houses."

Frank went on. "I think I know why this happens. Most agents believe this is a dead end—a waste of their time. Consequently, their attitudes and expectations are low. They think they're there to sell the house they are 'baby-sitting', and so they expect to participate in the numbers game. You know the *numbers game?* Sit on a house long enough and some poor lost soul will stumble into buying it. Well, that's 180 degrees from reality.

"My reality is that this house—the open house—is the *perfect* vehicle to practice your profession—and it's a darn fine profession, if I do say so myself!

"In my experience, numbers don't buy homes. People do. People who have hopes, desires, needs, and ... "

"And dreams," said Mar, finishing Frank's idea.

Mar's interest had peaked, but there were still some confusing issues and beliefs that Frank would have to confront, explore, and dispel before she could accept the open house as a credible playing field.

Frank continued. "It's not hard to book your entire month with open houses willingly given up by listing agents who neither see them as *diamond fields* nor appreciate the opportunity these open houses provide in maximizing their time and leveraging their talents.

"Once I recognized the diamond field for what it was, I often *volunteered* to run open houses for my associates, and they were delighted. And why were they delighted? Because they took the attitude that open houses are a waste of time. They saw them as a waste of time, while I and others saw open houses as a field of diamonds, or our *own personal diamond mines.*" Frank was careful not to offend Mar while he continued to pursue this direction of thought.

Mar needed to stop Frank for a moment. "Excuse me, Frank, but you keep referring to diamond fields and diamonds mines. I'm sorry, but I don't know the reference."

Frank appreciated Mar's self-esteem. He had learned over the years that secure individuals always speak up when they don't either understand or know something, just as Mar was doing. "Thanks for asking. It's a very interesting story, about the genesis of the diamond mines of South Africa, that many folks aren't aware of. And the gist of the story supports our discussion. I think this might be the time to relate this story that's been told and retold many times in the sales environment. In fact, it should add to our discussion. Let's see if you agree.

"About a hundred years ago in South Africa, a farmer was in town picking up supplies. As he walked out of the town's only dry goods store, he overheard a conversation that greatly interested him: Diamonds had just been discovered in a far off place in South Africa, hundreds of miles from his town.

"Finding diamonds in the late nineteenth century was akin to winning the lottery today—something you fantasize and day-dream about."

By this time, Mar had become fascinated by Frank's story-telling style and said, "Please, go on."

"Well, that evening the farmer thought long and hard about his own situation as he reheated half-week-old beans. Perhaps it was the news of newly discovered diamonds that became a catalyst for his introspective

thoughts—or maybe it was the beans!" Frank winked. "He was poor and struggling, with no clear prospect of seeing a way out of his dull, uneventful life. Yet now, he had a dream he could believe in—*finding diamonds*.

"Imagine, in one shovelful of digging, he could change his destiny and become somebody. Within weeks, this consuming passion, this fever, overcame him as it had thousands of others. In that short time, he could no longer face his daily chores nor contemplate another season on the farm. He *had* to escape. To prepare himself, he gathered as many provisions as he could and set out to find *his* diamonds.

"In his wanderings, he searched in every rumored area and remote field. Over the next seven years, he took odd jobs to keep going. In the end, he returned, a broken man, to his neglected, overgrown farm. He had found no diamonds and had wasted the last productive years of his life on a wild-goose chase. His desire for living had disappeared in his disillusionment with his luckless life. In one last act of desperation, he flung himself into his farm's drought-stricken riverbed and died," Frank's voice trailed off into silence.

"Frank, is *that* it?" asked Mar in amazement.

Frank's tale had sunk in for his companion. "Not quite," said Frank, welcoming the question and smiling a devilish grin.

"You see, Mar, the farmer who searched for his *very own diamond field* had gone looking for his fortune in far off places. The irony of the story is what happened *after* the farmer's death.

"Within a few months, a new owner took over. Not long after that, the new farmer stumbled upon strange looking crystals in the very riverbed that the first farmer had died upon. Curious about their origin, the second farmer brought them to town. To his astonishment, he was told by the local assay office that they were, indeed, diamonds—high quality stones of great dimensions and incalculable international value.

"In fact, the entire dried-up river bed was inundated with raw diamonds that could be scooped up by hand. This seemingly desolate farm eventually formed the basis for the DeBeer's diamond fortune and world empire.

"The poor hapless farmer had expected his riches to be elsewhere, but his *acres of diamonds* were under his feet all along!"

Mar was spellbound.

"Often, our fortune awaits us much closer to home than we imagine. I frequently reflect on this curious tale of irony because the message is compelling."

Mar now understood. Perhaps Frank was right. Maybe her own fortune lay in the open houses she had consistently ignored. After all, it was worth considering.

Mar's thoughts were interrupted by Frank's next comment. "Now you need to understand your role at the open house. This *is* your playing field because you are in charge of your fortunes ..."

At that moment, Mar couldn't contain herself any longer. "O.K., so this is your playing field. I'll give you that. But what happens on the field that makes it so special?" asked Mar.

"That's a fair question, Mar," said Frank, taking no offense at his young companion's eagerness and impatience. "Let me start painting a picture of what happens."

Frank continued. "You're politely talking with everyone who will talk to you. But not everyone will immediately open up to you. Don't be discouraged by this slow start. Remember, that's their 'surface stuff' showing. Many people will hold up a shield around themselves because they're fearful. In fact, some of the hardest folks to open up become some of the easiest folks to win over if you know what to look and listen for, what to ask for, and when to move closer to their shield to show them your product offerings."

"Frank, I want to take a step back for a moment and ask you a question. Why are they fearful?"

Frank took a moment to assess his earlier comment. He wanted to make sure that he had used the right word in its correct context. "I think I'll stick with the word fearful," introspectively remarked Frank. "Fear is the darndest thing. It not only gets us into trouble without us wanting to, but it has a way of blocking our real feelings from others and ourselves. Why people are fearful is pretty complex. After thirty years in the real estate business selling, training, and promoting new ideas, I'd have to say that the three most striking reasons for fear are these:

Three Reasons for Fear

1. SALES PHOBIA: Lacking information and being afraid of looking foolish in sales situations.

2. SHYNESS: Feeling uneasy in social situations.

3. CREDIT FEARS: Lacking confidence about the financial issues surrounding home purchasing or fearing being rejected for a mortgage.

"Mar, you'd be surprised how many people feel uncomfortable when it comes to finances. I've found over the years that the more straightforward the financial picture is, the easier for many people to commit to making a decision. In fact, if you remove that barrier, a new world opens up for most of your customers. Customers just don't believe that they can afford to step up to more house!

"In the old days, folks needed 10 to 20 percent down … but that's not the case today. Unfortunately, the word that this is no longer true hasn't gotten out. So what stops most folks today is just a smokescreen that drifts away once their financial path is understood. And this is one of your key success strategies in helping clients get into the home of their dreams.

"And from my observations over the years, Mar, our listening talents are another key strategy. Here's how I learned to listen in an effective way—and it's simple. Keep a notebook handy at all times to capture each prospect's comments, like a great reporter or interviewer almost always does. And, I might add, taking notes makes the other person see that what they're saying is important to you.

"You can pick up some terrific pointers by turning on *your* TV and observing the listening techniques the great interviewers have. You'll note that they aren't working with an agenda, and they don't turn the interview into a sermon or soapbox event. No, they ask an open-ended question and then shut up and wait for the answer." At that, Frank half-laughed, knowing that sometimes he was known for his sermonizing and he knew that was a no-no.

"You'll want to stay on point, courteously probe gently, and listen again. It's amazing what people will tell you if you let them. And this secret has been known throughout the ages. But for you it's invaluable because you'll be surprised how effective knowing some small tidbit is when you call your client back and they realize that you *listened to them.*"

"What do you mean, call them back?" asked Mar.

"I mean exactly that," said Frank. "What you're going to do is call each lead that you believe is remotely interested in either buying or listing in the future. Now, don't prejudge or assume anything. I don't care how gifted you think you are at reading other people's minds or interpreting their intentions. First impressions can be misleading and cost you a bundle. I know many people who have bought homes from me over the years who drove beat up cars and wore dirty old clothes, but who could buy and sell us both three times over.

"In short, *never* let appearances fool you or lead you to a conclusion. I'd say out of an open house, you'll generally find three to five credible prospects or even more than that if you're nonjudgmental and sharpen your listening and observation skills just a bit.

"O.K., now we're ready to get down to brass tacks."

Step One:

"Let's get into what you might say when you're calling a prospect back. An opening comment on the phone might be something like this: 'Good evening, Mrs. Smith. This is Frank Newman. We met at the recent open house for the Johnson's, who live right down the street from you. I'm from XYZ Realty and wanted to get back to you as I had promised. Is this a good time to chat for a moment, or am I interrupting something?'

"It's always a good policy to find out if you're interrupting them. Usually, whether you've intruded or not, they'll allow you 30 to 45 seconds to state your remarks, unless there's an emergency on their end of the phone. *Now, key to all this is to stop talking.* Say your piece and then let them speak. If you keep talking, it will turn them off; wouldn't it you?

"So, you might say something like this after they've responded. 'After you left the open house, your comment about *[blank]* was so interesting that it got me thinking about a property that I believe you'll really get excited about. It's in your price range, and I thought you and Mr. Smith might want to meet me on Wednesday or next Saturday and just take a look for the fun of it!'

"You'd be surprised how often an innocent comment can become a springboard to something exciting. You have used Mrs. Smith's comment to open the door to a relationship."

Step Two:

"Your next step is to listen carefully to Mrs. Smith's response. If it's at all positive, encourage both Mr. and Mrs. Smith to visit you. Always give your prospect two choices. By giving them two choices, you have allowed them to say yes. By giving them only one option, prospects will invariably pick a second option of their choosing. That option is, 'That date won't work.'

"When your prospect comes into your office to meet with you, I'd take them through the same steps used with a regularly motivated customer. As you can imagine, you can enjoy a continuous flow of self-selecting prospects using this technique. After all, if they have the motivation to meet with you, you're new clients have self-selected themselves without much fuss from your efforts."

Mar was amazed at the ease of Frank's explanation, and it fascinated her.

"Mar, let's do a little possibility thinking. If you were to attend four open houses a month and work with these prospects two

days per week, who knows what could happen with your business. I know many top producers who work as many as six to ten open houses a month, and their results keep them coming back for more. Now, the shake out on this is not only showing homes to these prospects, but in the listing opportunities you'll enjoy.

"This gets us to another crucial subject—*listing homes*. When you consider the existing school of thought—that cold calling and picking up expired listings are the way to kick-start your new business—I believe you'll find this new line of thinking and approach—*working the open house*—a productive opportunity hard to match and one that is hands-down superior to cold calling. In fact, if you work this way and get good at selectively identifying prospects, the idea of cold calling will be as alien as walking to Houston instead of flying!"

Mar laughed at Frank's analogy and her response was immediate. "Frank, in the past, I spent painful hours knocking on doors and sitting on the phone trying to list expired listings. Are you saying that I can stop my activity in this area—and cold calling for new listings altogether?"

"Yes and no," said Frank smiling.

"That sounds to me like you're waffling on my question," said Mar, poking some fun at her wise companion.

"I knew you'd pick up on that answer pretty quickly," said Frank, chuckling. "But here's why I said yes *and* no.

"Many successful agents have never cold called and they haven't picked up expired listings because they're *too* busy working with open-house prospects. What I'm telling you is that they are only mining half of the diamond field, when in actuality they could be listing from those other activities without too much trouble. So I hope that answers your question and removes me from being a candidate for waffling!

"Let's get back to the open-house prospect, because that's the key to this entire approach. In your conversation with the open-house visitors, you'll want to find out their thinking on how they'll be selling their existing home. My experience suggests that if these potential buyers are serious, then they should be open to the request to get their house on the market before they contemplate buying.

"Many markets fluctuate in the number of days the typical home stays on the market, but there is a pretty interesting rule of thumb on this one. As the price goes up by $100,000 chunks, say, from the $250,000 to the $350,000 price range, the number of days increases. So, an $800,000 home will normally take four times longer than, say, a $200,000 house, but of course, market conditions and regional differences make any generality risky at best. Still the basic equation stays the same and the essence of allowing you to list their home remains the key point to all of this.

"If your potential buyers are allowing you to show them their potential new home, it goes without saying that they *should be comfortable* discussing the sale of their present home. If this conversation—the pricing and marketing of their present home—creates an uncomfortable situation, then that's a warning signal that they're *not* yet serious about or comfortable with taking the next step. Or, it may simply be that a smokescreen of fear surrounding the financing issues still exists. So, in any case, I wouldn't ignore the issue of listing their present home."

Step Three:

"You should expect that after you've shown them three homes they will want to make an offer. You will be taking the couple back to your office so that they can pick up their car. When you're in your office discussing their offer ideas, you can very naturally state that you will draw up the offering document for them to review and sign. It is at this meeting that you will have them review and sign the offer, hand you their deposit check, and finalize the disposition of their existing property, if this has not been already done.

"For me, the key to listing has always been trust and full service. When you include these steps in the complete transaction, you're serving your customers needs most effectively. After all, who knows more about the entire transaction than you? Why expect your customers to buy a home from you and develop a relationship with someone else to sell their present home? Taking this approach of caring for the open-house prospect—helping them find their new home and aiding them in disposing of their existing property while shepherding them through the finan-cial maze—is the level of service and support they expect and need. What could be simpler?

"In summary, developing a trust level, or rapport, with people comes right back to your ability to meet their

hopes, desires, and needs, and it all starts with listening—listening to what *they* want and not being focused
on what *you* have to say."

By this time, Mar had finished her late breakfast and
was ready to fully converse with Frank. "It sounds too
easy, but I must say that I never saw the open house as a
prospecting platform. Rather, I was focused on selling
the open house while discounting all the Looky-Lous."

"You're not alone, my friend. In fact, you just
summed up why the majority of agents give no particular importance to open houses. If you see the open house
as your diamond field for selling and listing, then you
have dispelled a myth that has handicapped many an
agent—new and experienced.

"Before we move on, Mar, I'd like to give you a few
pointers on how to increase your opportunities for success at your next open house."

"I'm all ears," replied Mar.

Frank enjoyed Mar's enthusiastic response. "O.K.," he
said, "here we go.

"When planning for an open house, it's imperative
that you choose a home that's located in an easily accessible area, preferably close to a major arterial. The key
here is to select a home that's easy to find and one that
you can direct people to with the use of open-house A-
boards. When it comes to the use of open-house signage,
I strongly recommend overkill. The more signage, the
better! The key to a successful open house is to make it
an event. The more signs you have up, the more attention
you will attract to the property, something that hopefully results in more activity. Helium-filled balloons

attached to the signs are also effective in attracting the attention of passers-by.

"It's important to properly advertise and promote the open-house event. Your real estate office probably already advertises scheduled open houses in the local newspapers. In addition to this, you may want to consider running your own ad.

"Along with the newspaper ads, I would suggest that you either mail or hand deliver fifty to one hundred open-house invitations to residents in the surrounding neighborhood. Again, your real estate office probably already has addresses available. If not, your friendly title officer will be happy to supply you with the names and addresses you need.

"Once the invitations have been delivered, the next step is to get on the telephone and call the people you delivered invitations to. After inquiring whether they received an invitation, you once again extend the invitation to attend the open house, reminding them of the time and location. You might also mention that they may invite anyone else who may be interested in attending, such as a friend, relative, or coworker. While talking about the open house, you may find yourself talking to a potential prospect.

"If you find that attendance at your open houses is down, consider offering refreshments, such as hot dogs and sodas, at the next one. If you mention that you're serving refreshments in your advertisements and mail outs, you're sure to see attendance soar. In some instances, you'll probably need at least one other agent to assist you with the open house. Oftentimes your loan officer will be happy to help out with the refreshments so that you can concentrate on interacting with the prospects. I can remember one such event at a new home site that was so well attended I walked away with over a dozen new prospects.

"Remember to keep in mind at all times why you are hosting the open house. As you're visiting with each person, listen carefully to what they have to say. Make sure that you write down their names and phone numbers along with any comments they make. And don't forget to call them back within a day or two at the latest. There's bound to be someone in attendance who's planning on buying or selling a home, or both, in the near future."

Chapter Six

SIX

Follow Your Inner Voice

THUMBNAIL: An agent's focus must be on working with customers and prospects. The two major activities are meeting homebuyers' hopes, desires, and needs and listing homes. Ultimately, you must trust your inner voice for your strength. Stop following the crowd. Be bold, dream, and steer for "the second star to the right"!

Mar looked at her watch and realized that her time left with Frank was short. She knew that there was much to learn from him, and she wanted to make sure that her moments were well spent. "Frank, it seems to me that there is one other area that you haven't spoken to me about. As I think about this area, I can't help believing that there's a myth attached to it, but for the life of me, I can't imagine what it would be."

"What area is that?" asked Frank.

"It's what I call the paperwork," responded Mar.

"You mean the busywork," said Frank, smiling.

"Frank, it might be busywork to you, but without it, how do you keep your business going?"

"You've got a point there," said Frank. "It's not that you should ignore it. It's only that you need to keep it in perspective and guard against excess. I believe that

97

excess comes from following the leader—*a leader that oftentimes is following someone else*. Let me explain."

Mar knew that she was in for another one of Frank's wonderful stories.

"Several years ago a friend's uncle was retiring from an industrial plant in Toledo, Ohio. Ned Templeton was his name and this was his last day on the job. Ned had spent thirty-nine years at the plant and was retiring as the senior foreman on the day shift. Well, as my friend tells it, Ned decided to do something out of the ordinary that last morning. You see, for the past twenty-seven years, Ned had parked his car across the street from the plant's rear gate, where he always arrived a little after 5:00 A.M.

"Ned was an early riser, so getting up at this time of the morning was no sacrifice for him. As his tradition unfolded, just before going into the plant, he would take a moment and walk over to the window of an old clock-repairman's shop. Peering through the window, Ned would check his timepiece against the large grandfather clock standing just the other side of the front pane of glass. Ned would make sure that the time on his pocket watch matched the watchmaker's clock. For you see, Ned was responsible for the 6:00 a.m. shift, and the plant's whistle was the signal for everyone to shut down their work and let the next group take their place. At 12:00 noon, the whistle was blown a second time for lunch.

"In all the years that Ned had been responsible for the shift change and lunch break, not once had he thought about meeting the watchmaker. The clock shop didn't open until 9:00 A.M., and so he'd never had the time to step in and say hello. Today would be different, because

on his very last day on the job, his sole responsibility was to come to work and appear at his own retirement luncheon. So at approximately 11:00 A.M., Ned appeared at the rear gate with a few minutes to kill. For some reason, he decided to introduce himself to a stranger who had for over twenty years helped him keep the plant on schedule—*without even knowing it.*

"As Ned entered the watchmaker's world of clocks, he realized that the shop was much smaller than it looked from the outside and was crowded with all forms of timepieces. From small shelf clocks to large, standing floor models, the shop was cluttered and busy with mechanical ticking things.

"Ned took time very seriously and had earned a reputation for his dedication and commitment to its value in the workplace. He had always prided himself on his promptness, so he held great affection for these individual monuments to punctuality.

"Ned introduced himself to the old watchmaker. He explained how every morning at a little past 5:00 A.M. he had peered through the clockmaker's window, setting his watch to the grandfather clock in preparation for blowing the plant's whistle for the 6:00 A.M. shift change and the 12:00 noon lunch break.

"Instead of the quiet pleasure Ned expected to see on the face of the old watchmaker, he observed a serious and confused blank stare."

"Why was the old watchmaker confused?" commented Mar. "Didn't he understand what Ned was saying?"

"Yes, he understood what Ned was saying. It was *what* he said that confused the watchmaker. Please, let me go on with my story.

"At the sight of the confused stare on the face of the watchmaker, Ned inquired just like you, 'What's wrong?'

"As the watchmaker's expression changed to amusement, he began his explanation. 'For the past twenty-five years,' said the watchmaker, 'since I bought this shop from the previous owner, I've been setting my grandfather clock to the plant's 12:00 noon whistle!'

"The two men looked at each other ... then burst out laughing! For the past twenty-five years, both men had followed the other's lead without questioning the source of their blind faith. To both men, punctuality was an unspoken religion. And every morning each had paid homage to his false god.

"It would be just an amusing story if its application in so many ways was not so serious and apparent. Remember, you asked about paperwork. Well, paperwork is a false religion. How often I have observed my colleagues pouring over reports, comparative studies, comps, analyses, listings, contracts, and the like, when they should have been with prospects and customers and previewing homes.

"My observations over the past many years suggest that paperwork is over emphasized and over subscribed to. Like most nonessential activities, it is a never-ending struggle and an excuse to hide from our own success. *The more you do, the more you get trapped in a maze with no exit.* It seems as though every office has plenty of role models for this trap.

"The trend today is to hire others to do your paperwork, and that may be fine on the surface. To me, the key is to carefully examine each clerical task and make sure it's a necessary part of your business.

"Mar, here is something else to think about. I've often thought that part of the reason real estate agents hire assistants is to boost their egos. After all, having an assistant elevates our importance and communicates our success. How much more successful could these professionals be if they focused on the few areas that made them successful in the first place and judiciously requested limited help when they really needed it?

"In short, before you hire someone to help you with paperwork, make sure the paperwork is essential to moving your business forward. Invariably, we have a tendency to forget the things that make us successful. In this case, our success is predicated on consistently meeting with prospects, working with buyers, and finding ways to list homes.

"Handling every aspect of the business personally isn't critical to your success. And oftentimes, following others down the wrong road of over emphasizing paperwork isn't the answer either."

> MYTH NUMBER FIVE: You need to do lots of paperwork to be successful.

Mar interrupted. "Frank, I need a little clarity on this point. What are the things that I should do personally, what aspects of the business do you think I can delegate, and what part of the business is busy-work and *stuff* that I should abandon?"

"O.K., let's get to work on answering those three questions." At that, Frank grabbed his pen again and reached for a clean sheet of paper from his briefcase.

"Mar, I'm going to draw three headings on this paper: **Handle Personally, Delegate to Others,** and **Jettison/Stop Doing.**"

As Frank drew his chart, Mar realized that she was getting the first *real mentoring* she had received since starting in the real estate business.

Handle Personally	Delegate to Others	Jettison/ Stop Doing

"All right. I'm not going to do all the work on this one. I'm going to need your help. Why don't you fill in the first column and see how far we can get."

Handle Personally

"Well, first, I would start with the open house. I'd handle those myself," said Mar.

"Great," chimed in Frank. "What would come next?"

"Second, I'd handle the *follow-up calls* to attending open-house prospects.

"Third, I'd *make appointments* in my office to meet these prospects.

"Fourth, I'd *get my new customers financially qualified,* hopefully by putting them in touch with my lender.

"Fifth, I'd *ask* for *their home listing.*

"Sixth, I'd *show each customer three homes* that I believe they should consider buying.

"Seventh, I'd *help my customers arrive at an offering price,*" summarized Mar.

"Now you're cooking," said Frank, enthusiastically. "What about financially qualifying your prospects by delegating this activity?"

Delegate to Others

Task One: "Well, I'm going to connect with a mortgage broker who will do that, and I'm going to set that up beforehand," said Mar. "I'll find a mortgage broker who'll work when I do. You know, someone who'll be readily accessible to me and my customers."

"Exactly," said Frank. "So we would put part of financially qualifying under Delegate to Others.

"What about shepherding the buyer through the filling out of papers and the other qualifying administrative issues?" continued Frank.

"I'd delegate that to the mortgage broker. That's his or her job," said Mar. Frank was pleased with Mar's grasp of her duties.

Task Two: "O.K., what about workups on comparables for the listing price of your customer's existing home?" asked Frank.

Mar responded. "My best bet would be to delegate this task to another agent or administrative assistant. I'd, of course, review the information carefully and deliver it to my client, but I don't have to be intimately involved in the research. Then I would be involved in the final strategy and pricing after the information was gathered," said Mar proudly.

"Good thinking," said Frank.

Task Three: "O.K., what about expired-listing, for-sale-by-owner, and cold-calling activities? Have you made a decision about those issues?" asked Frank.

"Well, I think, without much counsel from you, I'd have to guess on this one: If I sharpen my open-house skills, I won't have to cold call or get involved in other listing activities. I would imagine that at some point in the future I might want to hire someone to cold call for me on both counts," said Mar.

"Yes, many of the more senior agents have one or two people whom they rely upon to make their cold calls. You must understand that in most communities, these channels are being worked pretty hard, and you may never want to get involved with this activity because the results ratio is low. It's perhaps something to consider at some point after you have become adept at your other skills.

"If you were just starting out, my advice would be not to invest either the time or money in this activity. As we all know, unsolicited contacts by phone and in person have caused an uproar at the national level. I foresee the day when phone-call solicitations will no longer be appropriate to personal residences."

Jettison/Stop Doing

"O.K., so you have a good handle on the first two columns. What about the last column, Jettison/Stop Doing?"

Mar was anxious to respond. "Well, if I remember the story about the grandfather clock, the watchmaker and Ned Templeton, and their following each other's lead, I'd stop looking for role models who are using the old paradigm and start using my own ideas. Otherwise, I'll again be buying into the myths of our business."

"Mar, you are a quick learner," said Frank, proudly. "That's exactly right. Those myths that we discussed will be great candidates for the third column. And over time, you should expect to add to this list other myths that become apparent."

Mar smiled and passed along the compliment. "Thanks, Frank, but I can't take all the credit. You're one heck of a teacher."

Frank couldn't resist focusing in on a subject now that was near and dear to him and introduced it into their conversation. "You know, I'm probably going to be accused of being old-fashioned and I've never been afraid of going against the popular current of ideas, but I suspect that most agents have forgotten two very valuable concepts in conducting their businesses."

Mar turned toward Frank to listen carefully to what he was saying and encouraged him to go on. "Frank, what might those concepts be?"

"The forgotten concepts are imagination and intuition. We have forgotten to use our creativity and guts in practicing our craft. I haven't heard the word imagination used in years in regards to our business. Maybe it's because we have become so suspicious of intuition and imagination that we shy away from these concepts. But I believe imagination is the one most invaluable ingredient missing in our business today. Everyone is afraid to take a false step, so we've systematically culled our agencies of imaginative dreamers. And yet, it is the dreamer who lights the paths we all follow.

"The great American philosopher Henry David Thoreau said, 'You have only to move in the direction of your dreams to meet with a success unexpected in common hours.'

"Likewise, Emerson told us to trust the voice within, to trust our own intelligence and the small still voice we so often fight to maintain false safety and the status quo.

"Mar, it takes a lot of courage to dream. But the rewards can be staggering. Nearly fifty years ago, Dag Hammarskjold, then Secretary General of the United Nations, said, 'Never, for the sake of peace and quiet, deny your own experience or convictions.'

"I believe those words are more important today than they were then. The path of least resistance is to go along with the group, entertain their vacuous humor, agree with their ideas and beliefs, and be one of the gang.

"It was the poet Robert Frost who warned of this drab path and painted for all eternity the alternative  path, 'the road not taken.' And the road less traveled leads to self-discovery. It wards off the disaster of finding that we have adjusted our clock to an expert no greater than ourselves and oftentimes much smaller."

Frank continued looking directly at his companion. "What direction will that take *you?* I'm not sure, but if you want a point of reference, perhaps the best advice was given by Peter Pan one hundred years ago when pointing out Neverland. He said with gusto, '*Second star to the right, and straight on till morning.*'" At that, Frank smiled a satisfied smile.

Mar realized that Frank was speaking from experience as he continued. "I believe that all these great people are talking about the human experience of going it alone, of finding our own way to serve others. I think that Emerson's inner voice is a voice we have all experienced. That voice is trying to tell us that what is good for us will be good for others. Our inner voice cries out for the fire of imagination in living our lives and conducting our business enterprises with courage.

"Mar, our business is simple. You and I serve others. Our service is to help buyers and sellers arrive at a fair and equitable agreement. The key is to regularly look at what we are doing and simplify our activities.

"Finally, my greatest advice to you is to guard against *following* the crowd. Chart your own course and creatively challenge the common thinking of others. If you decide to make real estate your career, it will be in this third column of our chart that your greatest challenges will appear."

Chapter Seven

SEVEN

The Greatest Gift Is Your Integrity

THUMBNAIL: We must depend upon our own good judgment and trust that inner voice. *When we do this, we unleash our creativity, imagination, passion, and integrity.*

As Frank spoke of ideals and concepts to live by, Mar could feel the plane meeting more resistance. She knew from experience that the pilot had increased the drag on the wings and that meant the plane was preparing to descend for landing. How enormously valuable her time with Frank had been. He had given her a new paradigm to consider, and he'd shown her a new practical direction to follow.

"You know, Mar, all this philosophizing leads us to one tried-and-true statement: We must depend upon our own *good judgment and trust that inner voice.* Perhaps that's too simple a concept in a complex world, but I believe it's the best advice I can give you. It's what I've lived by over the past thirty years, and it's kept me sleeping nights like a baby.

"In 1961, I read a book that I've always remembered. It was by Dr. Carl Rogers. It never made the bestseller list, but I found it impactful; and in his own right, Rogers was a visionary. In the book *On Becoming a Person*, Dr. Rogers outlined the characteristics of the new, emerging *ethical* person.

"Here is what he said over forty years ago about the different set of values this person will maintain and live by. 'I stressed,' he writes, 'their hatred of phoniness, their opposition to all rigidly structured institutions, their desire for intimacy, closeness and community, their willingness to live by new and relatively moral and ethical standards, their search for quality, openness to others' feelings, the need for spontaneity, their activism and their determination to translate their ideals into reality.'

"Back in 1961, Dr. Rogers was speaking about very few people. He was speaking about the 'change agents' of the future. That future is now! Rogers went on to say, 'When some part of a culture is decayed at the core, a small group with new views, new convictions, and a willingness to live in new ways, is a ferment that cannot be stopped.' Was he not talking about our individual passion, our unique needs and drives to regain our *authenticity?*" asked Frank.

Mar reflected aloud. "If I understand what you're saying, we can best prepare ourselves for the real estate business by becoming unique individuals who utilize our inner senses in responding to the challenges we face. And that our best preparation and response is to be ourselves ... be authentic and become our own change agents."

"That's exactly right. Slick, gimmicky, three-step closes, slam-dunk thirty-minute presentations, sandbagging pricing exercises, and manipulative sales tactics are not only dishonest, but are the quickest ticket to oblivion and self-loathing I know of. Authentic, high-integrity transactions, laced with a heavy dose of listening to your customers' hopes, desires, and needs, create the quickest and shortest line between you and success."

MYTH NUMBER SIX: The Sales Formula—You need lots of fancy training and high-pressure sales techniques to succeed.

"I guess you're really talking about another myth, aren't you?" responded Mar.

"We might be stretching it a bit, but it is quite evident that many of our colleagues believe that a *secret sales formula* is necessary to be effective, and it's not!" said Frank.

Mar could sense that Frank's demeanor had changed to a more somber tone as he continued. "Somehow, and with great sadness, I've seen a *shadow* loom over our industry. It's a sad commentary on our profession that we seek quick answers and easy solutions, when the real answers are self-reliance, integrity, perseverance, and imagination."

Mar seemed somewhat puzzled by Frank's words. "What do you mean, 'a shadow'?"

"I believe the shadow that has fallen over our industry is in the form of the quick fix, the newest trend, or the easy answer. We have only to pick up an industry newspaper or look through the junk mail in our offices to be astonished at the number of self-proclaimed experts *who in one day of training will turn our business around.* The fact is that the only person who can and should turn our business around is us."

"But, Frank, didn't you give me some fixes of your own?" asked Mar.

"Well, you might call them fixes, but I wouldn't. What I think I passed on to you were concepts and facts that dispel myths about our business. And once understood, accepted, and applied judiciously, these concepts create a new paradigm—one that keeps us in good stead for the long haul. The information that we've discussed is not a gimmick, a system, or a three-part solution. It's concepts that you should consider adapting to your style and approach of working in this industry.

"Let me see if I can put this all into perspective for you. Recently, when I was in the San Francisco Bay Area to teach a workshop on the concepts we've discussed here, a newspaper article caught my eye. It was a story about a famous retail chain whose humble beginnings began right after the Alaskan Gold Rush.

"The retail chain of stores' success was formulated on a simple and often forgotten philosophy—a philosophy, mind you, that doesn't include anything tricky or trendy. The basis for their phenomenal success stems from an adherence to *service*—gobs of exceptional, enthusiastic, uncommon service—as well as a dedication to award-winning quality in every product line they carry.

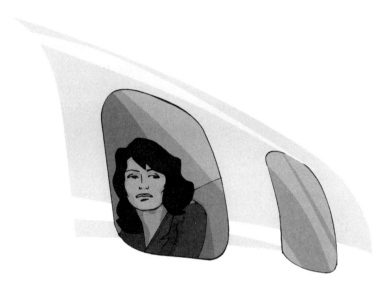

"In addition to this adherence to service and quality is anchored an unconditional guarantee of total satisfaction or your money back—*no questions asked*—on every product sold. And the results of their efforts? Outstanding financial performance."

Mar smiled broadly. "Frank, you must be speaking about my favorite store in all the world—Nordstrom. I wish I could shop there *all* the time."

"You bet. This retailer is in a competitive and crowded field of contenders. And they've been able to rise above the fray on these simple, time-honored concepts. Their buyers have specialized in identifying and gathering garments of the best available fabrics. Their focus has been on the upscale shopper, but the age-old principle held by the well-to-do is worth remembering and studying—*if you buy well and maintain well, you will save money in the long run.*

"Here is the really interesting part. When Nordstrom first announced that it would expand nationally, just about everyone in its industry believed that its simple and unaffected approach of trust, service, and quality would fail. Why? Because it was believed that certain parts of our country, unaccustomed to such levels of service, would take advantage of the money-back, no-questions-asked guarantee. Well, the experts were wrong, 100 percent dead wrong.

"Now, the substance of the article intrigued me for its truth and insights. The article stated that this retailer carried many of the same lines as its competitors in every market. But, for some unmistakable reason, people *preferred* to shop at Nordstrom—does that surprise you?"

"No, it doesn't," stated Mar. "I believe it's because of the way you feel when you're there, and that comes from excellent customer service and the way Nordstrom's employees treat each other.

Frank nodded. "In some cases, the article went on to say, its prices carried as much as a 20 percent premium and yet it had no trouble attracting and retaining loyal, enthusiastic customers.

"The article spoke about its magical ability to even do well in hard times. Imagine using the word 'magical.' Heck, there's no magic when it comes to providing exceptional service and quality products," said Frank.

"It's a success story that we can take to heart in our industry and learn much from, this often less-traveled road. This retailer's strategy remains simple. Should we not look at our own activities and simplify them to respond to the essential functions we perform?

"You see, in reality, buyers haven't changed. Sure, they may emphasize new or special needs, but their basic wants for home and hearth values remain constant. Purchasing a home is first and foremost *emotional*. Human emotions are relatively constant and unchanging.

"Mar, I'm convinced that once you've placed your customers in new homes that meet their hopes, desires, and needs, they'll come back to you to meet future hopes, desires, and needs as their families grow or their needs change as empty nesters. What better insurance policy for future business could you desire if you tastefully stay in touch?"

Mar was continually amazed with Frank's way of framing the obvious. Yet she was also somewhat embarrassed at how little of his down-home wisdom she'd experienced in her own broker's office. She flashed back to her office desk with the latest direct mail flyer promising in one day to teach her a new four-step process to increasing cold-call listings—one she had planned to attend. Now all that had changed.

"Frank, is there a way to briefly summarize what you've just said, so I can begin to incorporate your ideas into an action plan?" asked Mar.

"You bet. First, though, please understand that these *six* ground rules for success have been around for thousands of years. They're just not usually considered pizzazzi enough for the crowd, so they're unfortunately overlooked. Here is how I'd approach the six ground rules.

"I'd ask myself, **One:** What is the real value of my service? In other words, what function do I perform? And I'd include my broker's office and franchise in that answer.

"**Two:** Am I executing my service in the most straight-forward way possible?

"**Three:** Am I performing this service with integrity, and am I representing those properties that offer the best long-term value? Am I also resisting the temptation for the shortcuts, quick hits, and too-good-to-be-true sales?

"**Four:** Am I addressing the needs of my customers, and can I honestly say that this purchase or sale will be in *their* long-term interests?

"**Five:** Is the quality and value of the property understood by the buyer, including location issues, home design, and structural integrity?

"And, **Six:** Have I put the interests of both the buyer and seller before my own?

"Well, that about sums it up," concluded Frank.

"Wow, that's a pretty tough set of ground rules to follow," said Mar. "Can you make any money if you follow these six ground rules?" Frank looked at Mar with a wrinkled brow. "I'm just kidding you," said Mar, smiling.

"Boy, for a minute, you had me going," said Frank, with a relieved laugh. "You know, I didn't expect you to be overjoyed about these ground rules, hardly anyone ever is. After all, they ask a lot from anyone who wants to work in one of the hardest and most gratifying of all businesses.

"That reminds me of an old joke that goes something like this. A man asked another how many people worked at his place of business. After a moment's hesitation, the second man answered, 'Oh, about half!'

"You know, it seems as though unless people see the greater purpose in their lives, beyond the everyday, they work at less than optimum levels. Maybe that's natural or expected, but excellence never rears its head in that environment. It's only after we challenge ourselves that anything great is accomplished. I do believe that our greatest challenges come from within. Our greatest sense of accomplishment is also felt from within. Outside sources of approval are never really enough and they are not sustainable."

"I know what you mean," said Mar. "In just a few minutes, I'll have to give a full report to my dad on my progress."

"And how do you feel about that?" asked Frank.

"I don't feel great about it, and I know why. It's because I'm not doing as well as my dad expects."

"What about your own expectations?" asked Frank.

"Well, I'm pretty sure I've covered the details with you. I could be doing a great deal better than I am. And with what I've heard from you over the past several hours, I believe I'll be seeing some pretty impressive progress coming out of my new, more-focused efforts," said Mar, with great conviction.

Frank seemed pleased with his companion's proactive stance and expectations. "I'm glad you feel that way. People usually do after they've become acquainted with who is ultimately in charge of their success."

"I guess you mean me," said Mar.

"Right. You are the creator and recipient of your success. Get-rich-quick seminars and quick fixes are not the answer. Service, quality, caring, and relationships are the keys. And after spending this much time together, I believe you'll have no trouble at all."

"What do you think I should tell my father when he inquires?" asked Mar.

"Well, what do you think I'll say?" asked Frank.

"You'll probably advise me to tell the truth!"

Frank nodded approvingly and said, "Add the word *'unvarnished'* to it!" Both travelers laughed with understanding and a sense of satisfaction.

At that moment, the overhead address system interrupted them. *"Ladies and gentlemen, we shall be mak-*

ing preparation for our landing in Houston in a few minutes. Please see that your tray tables and seat backs are in their upright positions. Our attendants will be going through the cabin momentarily to pick up your empty glasses ..."

Mar felt energized by the day's meaningful conversation with Frank. She had expected an uneventful trip home and instead had gained a new lease on her career. How could she ever repay the gift that this stranger had bestowed upon her? As Mar turned to speak to Frank once again, he interrupted her thought.

"With your permission, I'd like to hear how you're doing over the next months. Perhaps you could drop me a line or two and fill me in on your progress. You know, I've got an investment in you now." At that, Frank's eyes twinkled with pride as he handed Mar his business card.

"Frank, how can I ever repay you for the gift you've given me?" asked Mar.

"Mar, your greatest repayment will come when you've not only succeeded with your own career, but when you've passed on these ideas and been an inspiration to others. You know, I'm very proud of our profession, and it's up to us ... you know what I mean," said Frank.

"Frank, you can be sure that I'll pass on this information to others. But first, I'm going to put these ideas into action when I get back home."

"Mar, the best advertisement for this information is to demonstrate its success. I'd make a small wager that your colleagues will ask what you're doing in a very short while. Then it will be your turn to share your knowledge. Knowledge *should* be shared!"

Mar had witnessed and experienced firsthand a sharing of knowledge for which she would be eternally grateful.

The plane's wheels thumped and skidded ever so slightly as they met the runway. Frank, smiling, looked at his watch and nodded in approval. "Well, we arrived in one piece and on time. Something to be grateful for."

When they reached the baggage claim area, Mar waved goodbye to Frank. He headed toward the taxi stand while she headed toward her parents. As he walked away from her, Mar was surprised that Frank looked smaller, more average than he had close up. Mar swallowed hard as she greeted her mom and dad.

Chapter Eight

EIGHT

Starting Over— Taking a New Approach to Selling

THUMBNAIL: *If we understand the six myths and the fundamental principles and ground rules behind them, we can enjoy a substantial income.*

In addition, we can invest significantly less time than we are presently spending and receive an enormous increase in personal satisfaction by serving *others.*

It was great to see her parents again. Mar hadn't been the best correspondent in the world, and her brief monthly phone conversations could not make up for the lost time. She felt lucky to have a good relationship with each of her parents, but the relationships were different; yet she knew that a bond of trust was always there. As they drove home from the airport, her dad's familiar aftershave permeated the car's interior. It felt good to be home.

"So, how's business?" asked Mar's father.

"George," her Mother scolded in a gentle way, "we have *plenty* of time to find out about Mar's new career before she leaves."

"That's O.K., I don't mind," said Mar, defending her dad. "In fact, I just had one of the most interesting plane rides of my life. Sitting next to me was a man by the name of Frank Newman, and boy, did he give me some things to think about," said Mar.

"You were sitting next to Frank Newman? Wow, he's one of the most well-respected real estate guys in America," said Mar's father. "People line up to speak to him, and you had several uninterrupted hours! I'd say you did pretty well for yourself, young lady."

Mar said, "He was so natural and unassuming, I didn't realize that I was sitting next to a famous man."

"Some of the most important people are unassuming," agreed Mar's mother. "Mar, you can't imagine how much we've missed you."

Once in the house, Mar excused herself and went upstairs to her old bedroom. She was glad nothing had changed since she'd left. Her life was the here and now, and her now wasn't so hot.

That evening after a delicious dinner, Mar's dad took the opportunity to ask about Mar's accomplishments. For the next half hour, Mar told her dad of her frustrations and thoughts about the past year's adventures in the real estate business. "I thought my first year in the Peace Corps was rough, but compared to the real estate business, it was a piece of cake."

"Did you get any tips or insights from Frank Newman?" asked her father.

"Tips or insights? You have to be joking! If I'm to believe Frank Newman, I'd say that I've been working the business all wrong and that I've wasted the last eighteen months of my life, especially since I'm almost through my savings and have little to show for it.

"But, Dad, that's the bad news. The good news is that if I use Frank Newman's concepts, then I expect to enjoy an increased income and accomplish more while working less hours."

"What did Newman say that makes you feel so confident?" asked her father.

"Literally everything he said made so much sense. Frank told me about the six myths of real estate sales. He said that agents have been passing these misconceptions on for years to new people like me in the name of 'helping.' He said they made up the old paradigm of the real estate industry."

"You know," said Mar's dad, "it only stands to reason that you'd have a few of your own in your industry. I'd be interested in what he said."

"Well, Frank outlined the six myths that support the old paradigm and shared with me some really new ideas on how to work the business. Let me tell you what he said. I hope I can remember it all."

At this point, Mar went over to her dad's desk, got out a yellow pad, and began her own seminar. She headed the page with ...

Six New Ideas That Will Change Forever The Way You Sell Real Estate

Then she told her father what she had learned and discovered as she wrote.

"**Myth Number One:** You won't make any money the first six months in real estate because you need lots of experience to earn a good income.

"**New Idea Number One:** You can begin to enjoy a strong income within the first forty-five to sixty days if you focus on one important element: Work with *buyers* every chance you get and don't defocus your efforts on other things.

"In addition, you may think that you need years in the business, but it just isn't true. Ninety percent of your prospective customers respond to your confidence, professionalism, and sincerity—not to the number of years you've worked in the business.

"**Myth Number Two:** You have to work very long hours, six and seven days a week.

"**New Idea Number Two:** Time is a precious commodity, one that has an integrity all its own. Respect its value and others will respect your time. Freely give your time and best efforts to those who deserve them. Guard your time jealously from those who regard it with little value.

"The best way to use your time is to listen to what other's say and observe how they behave. Pay attention to their comments, their body language, and what they don't say. A wise man once said that in every remark there is a *request*. Meet that request and you'll build trust, fulfill the hidden needs of your customers, and enjoy riches far beyond your expectations.

"**Myth Number Three:** You have to show buyers many houses before they can choose one.

"**New Idea Number Three:** YOU NEED TO SHOW PEOPLE NO MORE THAN *THREE* HOUSES! Driving people around and around until they find their 'dream' house is the wrong way to work. 'Serve people better, not longer.' In order to accomplish this, the following things should occur:

1. "Qualify your buyers in the office.
2. "Preview homes carefully and choose three to show your buyers.
3. "Show your buyers three homes—no more and no less.
4. "After showing your buyers three homes, they should be able to make a decision.
5. "If they cannot make a decision, you must let your buyers go.

"**Myth Number Four:** Open houses are a waste of time.

"**New Idea Number Four:** People who are present and future prospects for home ownership populate open houses.

"Once you acknowledge this, you've embraced a new concept and have exploded the fourth myth. In fact, open houses are a great source, if not the best source, for leads and listings.

"Many of the lookers are not ready to buy a home and are only there out of curiosity, but others are potential purchasers. Think of it this way: Not only will these people someday be buyers for homes you might want to sell them, but also they will need to sell their existing homes. Therefore, you have both dynamics—*buyers and sellers.*

"Myth Number Five: You need to do lots of paperwork to be successful.

"New Idea Number Five: Paperwork is over emphasized and over subscribed to. Like most nonessential activities, it's a never-ending struggle with our own initiative. Or put another way, it's a form of *creative avoidance.* The more busywork you get involved with, the more you get trapped in its maze with no exit. It seems as though every office has plenty of role models for this trap.

"Handling every aspect of the business personally isn't critical to your success. And oftentimes, following others down the wrong road of over emphasizing paperwork isn't the answer either.

"In addition, allowing inexperienced assistants to interface with your customers and listings is the quickest way to reduce trust levels and weaken relationships.

"Myth Number Six: The Sales Formula—You need plenty of fancy training and high-pressure sales techniques to succeed.

"New Idea Number Six: We can best prepare ourselves for the real estate business by becoming unique individuals who utilize our common sense in responding to the challenges we face. Our best preparation and response is to be ourselves, be authentic, and become our own change agents.

"Slick gimmicks, three-step closes, slam-dunk thirty-minute presentations, sandbagging pricing exercises, and manipulative sales tactics are not only dishonest, but are the quickest ticket to oblivion. Authentic, high-integrity transactions, laced with heavy doses of paying attention to our customers' hopes, desires, and needs, create the shortest line between us and success.

"**One Final Thought:** The forgotten concepts are imagination and intuition. We have forgotten to use our creativity and gut in practicing our craft. The word imagination hasn't been used in years in regards to the real estate business. Maybe it's because we've become so suspicious of intuition and imagination that we shy away from these concepts.

"Imagination is the *one* most invaluable ingredient missing in our business today. Everyone is afraid to take a false step, so we've systematically culled our agencies of imaginative dreamers. And yet, it is the dreamer who lights the paths we all follow."

As Mar completed her impromptu seminar, she felt a surge of energy. Her father could sense her intensity for the subject, and he was beaming from ear to ear.

At that moment, Mar's mom broke the silence in the room by quietly entering. "George, it's getting late. Maybe you and Mar can continue your talk in the morning."

George winked at Mar, as though they had a kept secret. "Mar and I have concluded our talk about her business, and I'm very encouraged by what I've just heard. I think Mar is going to make a success of her business and I couldn't be more pleased." At that, he touched Mar's hand lightly and smiled at her.

Upstairs in her old room, Mar opened her suitcase and felt a sense of calm and security. She wasn't sure whether it was from being back in her childhood home or because she now had a powerful strategy to launch when she returned to New Jersey.

As Mar's head touched her pillow, she could not help but hear Frank's voice whispering to her:

"We must do our preliminary homework better to serve better. We must learn to see with our ears as well as our eyes. We must be dedicated to our customers' wants and needs, rather than be motivated by what *we* want and need. We must truly become a servant of our customers' interests by listening to what they have to say and not being so interested in what we have to say."

Even in her drowsiness, Mar knew her journey had begun ...

EPILOGUE

Thanks for joining us. We had a lot of fun sharing these six *new* ideas with you and introducing you to the new paradigm for selling residential real estate.

By now, we know you have recognized the underlying element most significant for Phil Gerisilo's success. It is not just solely using these six new ideas, but *his joy of serving others.*

If you've enjoyed the story and its message, we invite you to pass this book on to a friend.

Thank you!

Succeed in Real Estate Without Cold Calling!

"Jump-start to Success with Phil Gerisilo!"

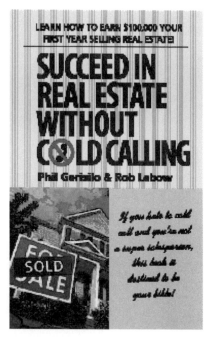

To learn more about how Phil achieved great success so quickly in Real Estate sales, join him personally at one of his North American seminars to jump-start your career!

TAKE-AWAY CONTENT!

One—Explode the six myths of Real Estate sales and succeed using six new ideas!

Two—Take advantage of a complete *marketing system* outlined in this exciting seminar!

Three—Learn a new approach to *time management!*

Four—Use *open houses* as a launching pad!

Five—*Create a never-ending river of new clients without cold calling!*

Six—Build a *bulletproof database* of repeat and referral clients!

Seven—Build a *strong support team* that is committed to your success!

Eight—Learn how to only *work with people you like!*

Nine—*Make more money* in less time and with a lot less stress.

Ten—Create a real estate business that *you can later sell or turn over to your children!*

- By attending this "packed to the gills seminar," you will learn how to enjoy the real estate business by becoming a great listener while finding the real joy in serving others.

- By attending this seminar, you will learn the specific skills and philosophy you need to succeed in Real Estate sales while maintaining a balanced, joyful life.

From a dead start and with no formal training, Phil developed a simple approach to selling homes. His experience comes firsthand. This is truly a sales revolution for all Real Estate sales people.

Come join us and spend time with Phil personally!

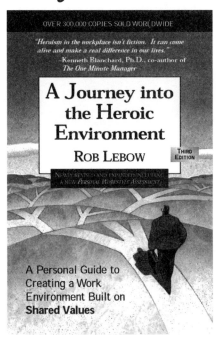